TASTE OF DARTMOUTH

OVER 50 RECIPES FROM DARTMOUTH'S TOP CHEFS

FOREWORD BY JOYCE MOLYNEUX
PHOTOGRAPHS BY DEBBIE JONES & PHIL SCOBLE

RAISING FUNDS FOR
Dartmouth Caring
Supporting Our Community

Dartmouth is now a 'foodie' destination, famous for its award winning restaurants and annual Food Festival. This book captures all the flavours and atmosphere of this culinary town, featuring its top chefs and over fifty of their delicious recipes.

Joyce Molyneux, of 'Carved Angel' fame, says in her Foreword:
"I would like to give a warm welcome to this collection of recipes from chefs working in Dartmouth....they have kindly donated them to this book which is being sold in aid of the local charity, Dartmouth Caring; an organisation which is a bridge between the medical profession and the needs of Dartmothians."

Enjoy the Taste of Dartmouth and help those in need of care.

Bon appetit...!

Published in association with
Dartmouth Caring
Supporting Our Community

Richard Webb, Dartmouth
www.dartmouthbooks.co.uk

CONTENTS

PHIL SCOBLE

Coming from a press background, Phil has always enjoyed taking pictures of people most – though any subject can fire his imagination.

Living and working in Dartmouth he sees the good work that Dartmouth Caring does each and every day in the community, and so is very pleased to be helping them raise funds through this exciting and unique book.

He has been delighted to be invited into the restaurants of the area's best chefs, and find an image which captures something of their personality and skill.

Website: www.philscoble.co.uk

DEBBIE JONES

An experienced and respected photographer, Debbie's passion for food is at the core of her business Imaging Essence.

Since the family home was relocated from Cardiff to Dartmouth in 1996, Dartmouth has pretty much become Debbie's second home especially as she spends so much of her time based at the furthest point away from the sea!

The fabulous support and services that Dartmouth Caring brings to the local community is essential and she was delighted to be able to support its good work by donating photography usage for "Taste of Dartmouth".

Website: www.imagingessence.co.uk

First published in the United Kingdom in October 2011 by Richard Webb, Publisher
Designed by Shillabeer Design, Dartmouth www.shillabeerdesign.co.uk
Text, Design and Chef photos © Copyright 2011 Dartmouth Caring
Front cover photo © Copyright 2011 Phil Scoble
Food Festival photos © Copyright 2011 Dartmouth Food Festival
Ingredients photos © Copyright 2011 Debbie Jones/Imaging Essence

A CIP catalogue record for this book is available from the British Library
ISBN 978-0-9568464-1-9
Printed and bound in the United Kingdom by Kingfisher Print & Design, Totnes

Richard Webb, Publisher, Dartmouth, Devon, England
www.dartmouthbooks.co.uk

The idea for this book came from David Jones (Manna from Devon) in February 2009 and it has taken us all this time to develop and produce it. There are so many people I have to thank, David, for his wonderful idea and his inclusiveness of allowing us to launch the book at Dartmouth's 2011 Food Festival, all the chefs for their contribution and Phil Scoble for his hard work in composing the profiles of the restaurants and chefs, Nick Shillabeer who has created the design and graphics and our main contributor, Joyce Molyneux. Without Joyce's help and support this would not have been possible. She originally offered to do the Foreword but in the end has edited all the menus. My sincere thanks to this wonderful lady. My thanks also to Richard Webb who has not only published this wonderful book for us but helped us bring it all together at the end to create the book you see here today. Lastly my thanks to the team in the office Alison, Karen and Katherine, not only for getting all of the parts of this book written and together but for managing to continue the important work with our clients and services at the same time.

Dartmouth Caring is a small charity serving the local community and we are totally reliant on donations to survive. I have to express my sincere thanks to all the chefs for contributing to this book and all the proceeds will go to the charity. Though we are a small charity we respond to the local needs of the community with particular emphasis on the vulnerable and elderly. We work very closely with the Medical Practice and healthcare professionals in our locality. We hear so many stories of people whose parents live in other parts of the country and the facility Dartmouth Caring offers is not available to them. We are saddened by this and it reinforces for the team and the trustees of the charity that we are obviously doing the right thing. We live in a wonderful part of the country and we are extremely lucky to be part of a community that is supportive. 35% of Dartmouth's population is over 65 and 20% is over 85 therefore you can see that our services can be utilised. We offer a comprehensive package to clients and because we work so closely with healthcare professionals in the area very few people fall through the net. Our main philosophy is that if people wish to remain in their homes then we try to ensure that this happens for as long as possible. We work very closely with clients and their families and all the feedback we receive is very much appreciated.

I would like to thank you for buying this book and assure you that all the donations go directly to helping us in our work.

I do hope you enjoy the recipes included.

Best wishes

Dee Nutt
Chair
Dartmouth Caring

'In no part of England are kitchen-gardens laid out on a more extended scale, or to better purpose. They abound with wall fruit of the finest quality; and all kinds of vegetables for the table are equally excellent and abundant.' So wrote the Reverend Thomas Moore in his History of Devonshire in 1829. We have long lived in an area blessed by climate and hard work which produces the materials of cookery in god-like plenty. Dartmouth, of course, had a certain problem accessing this plenty before the days of petrol engines and pneumatic rubber tyres. The road system was exiguous and the hills were steep. Most supplies came in by water and this might not be a long-term inconvenience but would pose problems for the daily shopping. So the town in many respects was pretty self supporting, and inward looking too for the outside visitors that grew inexorably in number during the reign of Queen Victoria, tended to concentrate on better-known pleasure resorts such as Torquay, Teignmouth and Paignton. But at the same time the small population of our town was provided with two inns and twenty-one taverns and another dozen beer houses. There were, furthermore, twenty-one bakers, a big brewery at Warfleet, a mineral water manufacturer, a ginger beer maker, three wine merchants and a cider merchant. At the outbreak of the First World War there was a tripe dresser working in the market and nine butchers in the town.

So in some ways we have passed from plenty to starvation in little more than a century, as the number of people devoted to our food supply (and beverage, lest we forget) has reduced and concentrated into a handful of international supermarkets and traders, together with a tiny number of independent shopkeepers.

Strange to say, at the same time there has been a vast increase in the number of restaurants, hotels and public houses devoting their working days to providing cooked food for residents and visitors alike. In those far off days of Queen Victoria there were of course no restaurants and few eating houses. The first reference to a stand-alone eating house that I have found is in 1852 in the care of Betsy Rawl, and then in 1866 there were dining rooms in the care of George John in Duke Street and a refreshment room in Foss Street run by Abiezar Rowe. The first restaurant, so called, was not recorded until 1893 when a confectioner on the quay called James Charles Dawe began what became the Criterion Restaurant, now Taylor's. There is no other mentioned until 1914 when Miss Helena Harris ran the Alexandra Restaurant on South Embankment. There was, of course, The Royal Castle, which had been the premier inn for many a year, as well as another called the London Arms in Foss Street. But the growth of hotels like that of restaurants came right at the end of the Victorian era, and their establishment was connected with the new developments in the town up Victoria Road and along the river on the Embankment. The most interesting development of that time was the great increase in temperance establishments. The Raleigh Hotel on South Embankment was in fact a temperance hotel and I have noted Mrs Ann Couch's temperance coffee rooms in Victoria Road, as well as The Dartmouth Coffee Tavern and Temperance Hall run by the YMCA. (It should be noted, in parenthesis, that Dartmouth was a town renowned for its drunkenness. Hard labour and salt air provoked many to slake their thirst deeply in beer and cider, to the horror of the magistrates it should be said).

All this was to change after the Second World War and even as late as the 1960s when the maritime trade of the port somewhat reduced,

the number of holiday visitors vastly increased, yachtsmen moved wholesale into the river, and England learned to love a restaurant. When I first came down to Dartmouth at the end of 1973, those pioneers of the '60s renaissance still survived: Leon's Bistro, The Tall Ships, and (where we were to start The Carved Angel) Glenie's. At the same time as we began on South Embankment, Jeremy and Diana Taylor were opening their restaurant overlooking the Boat Float. But we barely imagined how in the ensuing thirty years the restaurant ecology of the town would change. I recall winter weeks when we might see a bare half-dozen customers from one weekend to the next. Nowadays the clatter of knives and forks and the ringing of glasses can be hard in every street on every single night. It can't be bad can it?

25 years in business has given Pat Candy a real understanding of kitchenware - but her expertise is, she says, more down to her passion for cooking.

'I love to cook - I certainly seem to have lots of people who want to come to dinner so I can't be that bad!' she said.

The Kitchen Shop at the end of Foss Street was opened by Joyce Molyneux - and Pat says that a great professional like Joyce instinctively understands the need for good cookware.

'Buying the best kitchenware is an investment - and you get better results when you invest in good quality,' she said, leaning over the counter in her shop which is crammed with the world's most renowned cookware, yet has the feel of a corner shop.

Pat is not only an accomplished cook and store keeper - she is an expert on cookware and cooking equipment.

In fact, such an expert is that Sabatier, the most-famous of all the world's knife manufacturers, asked her to testify about cheaper copies of the knife which were proliferating a few years ago.

'I thought it was a joke when they called me,' she said. 'It was very flattering to get the call. In the end I never did testify as they decided to sell licences to all the manufacturers who were copying them - there are more than 20 now.'

She also suggested a need for a Tarte Tatin dish to one of her suppliers - Silverwood - because she and her customers needed one. The manufacturer made it, sold it to her and found that they had orders pouring in - the dish still sells thousands each year.

In 25 years things have changed a great deal in cookware, but some things always stay the same.

'When I started Le Creuset was the one everyone wanted - and they are still great. But the German manufacturers have really started to come into their own now, and some of them make the most amazing stuff. I've never been much of a gadget fan, although there are some great items to help around the kitchen. If you have the basic mix of equipment - a good quality set of pans, knives and other essentials, you can create anything.

'I try and ask what kind of heat people are using, as it changes what is best to use. In the last few years induction - using magnetism to cook with - has become very popular because it is instant and safe.

'If you want to use the best, you do have to pay more, but if you think of the value of the food you will put in that pan, in just six months, and how much you will enjoy that food if it is cooked well, it's not much of a cost - a good set of pans and knives will last you a lifetime.'

FOREWORD BY JOYCE MOLYNEUX

I would like to give a warm welcome to this collection of recipes from chefs working in Dartmouth hotels, restaurants and bistros. They have kindly donated them to this book which is to be sold in aid of the local charity, Dartmouth Caring; an organisation which is a bridge between the medical profession and the needs of Dartmothians.

Each establishment has given 3 recipes associated with a season, and a short description of the business giving a flavour to the reader. I enjoyed this flavour of the character and purpose of the hotel, restaurant or bistro.

This would have been a much slimmer volume when we opened The Carved Angel in 1974. It reflects the growth in popularity of eating out, once a special occasion or family celebration, now it is part of everybody's routine.

Dartmouth shows its best face in the summer, but winters can be quite severe with a cold easterly wind. Then it is time for the "winter" recipes, baked camembert, a beef and porcini suet pudding, venison sausages, braised pig cheeks and treacle tart. "Spring" means freshness so asparagus and nettle soup or the sharpness of poached rhubarb with creamy rice and spring rack of lamb. Paella is "summer" for me with Brixham crab in all its forms. "Autumn" means the arrival of game and I welcome wild ducks, pheasant and venison with perhaps the odd woodcock. We were lucky to have game years ago from Humphrey Harvey's shoot nearby, wild ducks first then pheasants came in perhaps a few partridge, a lovely woodcock. Through his good offices we also had a few grouse from Scotland which arrived with heather flowers in their crop.

Reading the recipes reminds me of how lucky we were to have many local suppliers, whether small businesses or self employed. Local fishermen who brought in their catch, either shellfish or wetfish as well as the small fishmongers who bought for us on Brixham market. Those early days we had Dart salmon brought in by a licensed netter. We used several butchers in Dartmouth and Totnes.

I also remember fondly the several owners of Dittisham Fruit Farm and the time when the market grocer sold local hothouse Muscat grapes. All the lovely local fish mentioned in the recipes pollack, slip soles, bass, scallops, crab, plus fresh crab and sprats in the autumn are great. Mackerel too is a beautiful fish and the best place to eat it is as close to the sea and as fresh as possible – simply grilled with a sharp sauce like apple or gooseberry, but it's also good with paprika or chilli and ginger with the richness of the fish in mind.

I hope you enjoy the book, the recipes are designed for family use adapted from the chef's restaurant ones. Armed with your Dartmouth Caring Cookery Book you can do a tour of the town popping in for refreshment as needed. Then take a sharp walk up Jawbones and enjoy one of the best views of Dartmouth away from the crowds. Eventually go home and cook something delicious from the cookery book.

ANZAC STREET BISTRO

Anzac Street, Dartmouth, Devon TQ6 9DL. TEL: 01803 835515

CHEF SERIN AUBREY

"I was born and raised in Kent but when I was only one my Dad decided to buy an old farmhouse and 30 acres just outside Blackawton and planned to take early retirement and live the good life. The farm is quite a different place now 350 acres and over 1,000 breading Ewes. The farm is run by my older brother Peregrine and we grow and produce ingredients for the bistro.'

'My career started when I was lucky enough to win a Conran Scholarship and went to London to learn at the best school with a guaranteed job with Sir Terance Conran on graduation. I worked in a few of his restaurants but ended up at his then flagship restaurant Le Pont De La Tour overlooking Tower Bridge. It was a great time of my life, I learnt lots and got to cook for the rich and famous: the pinnacle being a visit from then president Bill Clinton. I spent all my spare time in Devon when it dawned on me that it would be a much better idea to live and work in Devon and visit London than the other way round. At first I helped on the farm before the Bistro came on the market and the journey began.'

'We have worked hard to build up a good reputation and I am very proud of what we have achieved. I often get asked why do I do it and do I still enjoy it and the answer is always the same. I do it because I love to make people happy. I get a real buzz out of seeing people leave my restaurant happy, grinning from ear to ear. With more than a decade of success under our belt we have established ourselves as one of Dartmouth's favourite restaurants. Our menus change regularly to make best use of fresh local ingredients, seasonal produce and the ever-changing fresh fish availability. A lot of our dishes are classic French but utilising all the best local produce with a few foreign twists. It makes perfect sense as the French take their food very seriously and we share a very similar climate and lots of our produce is very similar.'

STARTER - WHITE BEAN & TRUFFLE SOUP

METHOD

Take a heavy bottomed large sauce pan and start to heat, add the butter and let it start to sizzle now add the onion, carrot, leak, garlic, thyme, parsley and truffle oils. Fry until the vegetables have softened but not coloured.

Now add the soaked beans and chicken stock and simmer cook until the beans are tender, this will take between an hour and an hour and a half. Take the soup off and allow to cool a little then start to purée the soup in a blender. If you're going to serve it straight away re-heat in a saucepan seasoning with sea salt and black pepper to taste adding the double cream making a creamy thick yummy soup.

Serve in a bowl with the truffle oil swirled on top.

INGREDIENTS - serves 4

1. 150g haricot or cannellini beans, soaked in cold water overnight
2. 6 cloves of garlic
3. 1 large onion, peeled and quartered
4. 1 carrot, peeled and roughly diced
5. 3 celery sticks roughly diced
6. 1 sprig each of thyme and parsley
7. 2 litres chicken stock
8. 100g unsalted butter
9. 200ml double cream
10. 1 tbsp truffle oil, plus extra to drizzle

INGREDIENTS - serves 4

1. 4 lamb racks

2. 1 small or half a large red bell pepper

3. 1 small red chilli deseeded

4. 2 cloves garlic

5. 1 tsp chopped mint

6. 1 tsp ground coriander

7. 1 tsp ground cumin

8. 1 tsp saffron threads

9. 2 tbsp olive oil

10. Salt and black pepper

METHOD

Trim away most of the fat and all of the membrane covering the eye of the meat. Season with salt and pepper.

Chop the bell pepper, chilli, garlic, mint and spices together until the mixture is almost a pulp. Stir in the olive oil, and then rub this mixture into the meat. Wrap the coated racks in cling film and place in the fridge for 2-3 hours.

To cook heat the oven to 200°C, gas 6. Heat a dry frying pan then working with one at a time add the racks and cook until sealed on the outside. Transfer the racks to a roasting tray and cook in the oven until pink around 10 minutes. Leave the racks in the tray to rest for a few minutes before serving. The pan juices will make an excellent sauce when simply poured over the meat.

METHOD

Stage 1

We serve these in 100ml petit pots but espresso cups or small ramekins would work well.

Bring the cream and milk up to the boil careful not to let it boil over and add the shot of coffee. In a separate bowl have the egg yolks and sugar mixed and ready, pour over the cream and milk mix whisking the two together at the same time. Return the mix to the saucepan and continue to cook over a low heat until the mix coats the back of a spoon.

Pour into the pots and allow to cool then chill in the fridge; they will now set in the pot.

Cover a baking tray with baking parchment.

Stage 2

Pour the water into a saucepan then add the sugars syrup and butter bring these to the boil and cook until small cracks appear at a temp of 135°C, gas 1 when it will be a rich golden colour. Add the bicarbonate and this will make the mix bubble like crazy and go light and airy. Now pour the mix onto the parchment and allow to cool and harden. You can keep and store this in an air-dry tin.

To serve put a thin layer of double cream on top of the chilled coffee mix and then grind some honeycomb on top and a few pieces on the side.

INGREDIENTS - serves 4

Stage 1

1. Half pint double cream
2. Half pint milk
3. 1oz sugar
4. 7 egg yolks
5. 1 double espresso shot

Stage 2

1. 2 tbsp of water
2. 225g Demerara sugar
3. 225g granulated sugar
4. 50g golden syrup
5. 15g unsalted butter
6. 1 tbsp bicarbonate of soda

BROWNS RESTAURANT

27-29 Victoria Road, Dartmouth, Devon, TQ6 9RT.. TEL: 01803 832572

CHEF JAMES BROWN

Browns Hotel Dartmouth is a small, stylish townhouse hotel, restaurant and bar in the centre of Dartmouth. Run by James and Claire Brown, the smart, contemporary furnishings and unstuffy atmosphere make Browns Hotel an ideal place to relax and enjoy the spectacular South Hams coastline.

James said: "We like to buy our food from small local producers and suppliers. Approximately 80% of our food is produced or sourced within South Devon. We have a thread of Spanish flavours that permeate our menu. Obviously these foods can't be local, but we buy the majority from Brindisa, who are renowned for their use of small family artisan producers, just the sort we like to use here in the South Hams!

"We like to think our food is packed with flavour. This is more important than fussy presentation. We like our food to be relaxed and casual, that's

not to say we don't try quite hard, but our house speciality is unfussy Paella! We make all our ice-creams, breads, chutneys, jams, stocks and sauces.

"We hang our steak a little longer than most and insist on it being dry aged which we know costs a bit more, but we think makes a difference. Our bacon comes from just over the hill and arrives with farmer Jilly Rowden each Friday. Most of our fish comes from Mark Lobb who must be unique as a sole trader at Brixham fish market. We normally buy what is cheapest because that's what is most plentiful and therefore in season.

"For crabs and mussels we use Moby Nick's Dartmouth shop. We're not too keen on farmed fish so if we want to make Gravadlax we make sure we buy the salmon from people who farm less intensively. Our salads and many of our vegetable choices are grown by Paul at South Pool Farm."

METHOD

Mackerel is a sustainable fish and available all the year around. This salad is bursting with flavour and if you can make the effort to smoke your own you will elevate this salad to new heights. Once mastered the basic smoking technique can be used on all sorts of food.

To prepare the mackerel fillets. Submerge the fillets in a brine (1 litre of water, 125g of table salt). Small fillets will need 3 minutes, large fillets 5 minutes. Remove from the brine and rinse in fresh water, pat dry, then leave on a baking rack to dry further, until they are slightly tacky, about 1 hour.

In an ideal world you would hot smoke the fillets for 1 hour at a low heat of about 100°C, not even gas 1. This will ensure that the mackerel is moist with a soft texture – and quite different from super market bought smoked mackerel! You are probably going to use a BBQ with flavoured smoking chips so go slowly and watch the heat!

When the fillets are cool, gently pull the flesh apart and combine with all the other ingredients lightly. So simple!.

INGREDIENTS - serves 6

1. 1 bag of mixed leaf salad
2. 1 medium raw beetroot - julienned
3. 1 small fennel bulb thinly sliced
4. 2 hard boiled free range eggs, quartered
5. 1 apple cut into thinly sliced wedges
6. 4 small or 2 large fillets of mackerel brined and hot smoked or supermarket smoked mackerel
7. French dressing made with cold pressed rapeseed oil (available from supermarkets) not olive oil.

INGREDIENTS - serves 6

1. 250g Bomba Paella rice (search it out and pay more; it makes a difference!)

2. 1 cup sofritto (1 large spanish onion, 2 fresh bay leaves, 6 chopped cloves garlic, 1 g saffron)

3. 1 tsp Smoked Paprika, salt and course black pepper

4. 2 free range chicken thighs, deboned and roughly chopped.

5. 2 soft cooking chorizo sausages, sliced – preferably from Brindisa.

6. 24 local mussels

7. 400g local fresh (not frozen) squid. Score the inside of the body sac, reserving the tenticles. Cut into strips.

8. 24 whole uncooked North Atlantic prawns

9. 100g peas.

10. Chopped flat leaf parsley

11. Lemon wedges (to serve)

METHOD

Paella is our signature dish at Browns. In order to perfect a method that allows us to serve it to order for a single person we have had to break a few rules! However with care you can capture all of the flavours you would expect from a paella without the specialised equipment you normally associate with this dish. The secret is in the preparation and the choice of first class ingredients.

This recipe does not use stock. Most of the preparation can be done up to a day in advance! To compensate for the lack of stock you need to carefully build up the layers of flavour and use the best ingredient you can find. The core of a paella is a good sofritto. Chop the onion and cook very slowly in a frying pan with the other ingredients for an hour, at which point you will have a fragrant yellow sofrito. Reserve. Wash the rice and then add to a saucepan of salted boiling water and cook for 8-10 minutes until it is al dente. Drain and immediately refresh in cold running water until it runs clear. Reserve. Cook the chicken in a frying pan until it is cooked through. Reserve until you are ready or continue on with the rest of the paella.

When you are ready to make the paella place the chopped chorizo in a large frying pan or wok and cook until the chorizo is starting to colour and has released its juices. Add 1/4 of a tsp of smoked paprika per person – do this 6 times to get the quantity right! Add 6 pinches of salt and 6 of black pepper. Now add the sofritto and the chicken with all the juices or jelly and thoroughly combine. Now add the rice and thoroughly combine. Now add the remaining ingredients and thoroughly combine. You want to cook this on a high heat with a lid on your wok or frying pan. Every couple of minutes thoroughly recombine. Turn the heat to medium after 4-5 minutes. The paella is ready when the mussels have opened and the prawns are cooked through which should be after about 15 minutes. Don't worry if you burn the bottom a little – this is the best bit!

Divide into 6 plates and serve with wedges of lemons. Enjoy.

METHOD

The perfect dessert – runny in the middle every time!

Melt the butter and chocolate in a bowl over simmering water. Beat the eggs and sugar together. Slowly add the chocolate mix to the beaten eggs, whisking all the time. Gently fold in the flour until well combined. Prepare 6 or 8 3 inch wide ramekins by buttering the inside and then dusting with cocoa powder. Fill the ramekins 3/4 full. You can now chill in the fridge for up to 3 days. To cook, transfer to a hot oven 180°C, gas 4. The fondants are cooked when the mixture forms a perfect dome. This will take between 10-15 minutes. It is the dome not the time that is important! Ease a knife around the edge and quickly tip into your hand (use a clean tea towel) before plating with the dome uppermost. Serve with a scoop of ice cream.

INGREDIENTS - serves 6-8

1. **250g butter, cubed**
2. **250g good quality chocolate**
3. **6 whole eggs**
4. **6 yolks**
5. **145g sieved plain flour**

MANNA FROM DEVON

Fir Mount House, Higher Contour Road, Kingswear, Devon TQ6 0DE. TEL: 01803 75294

CHEFS HOLLY AND DAVID JONES

Manna From Devon is an award-winning cookery school on the Kingswear side of the River Dart. Run by David and Holly Jones, the school specialises in fish, bread, Mediterranean, Asian, wood-fired oven and family courses using the best local ingredients the South Hams has to offer.

The school offers small hands-on courses throughout the year much enjoyed by students as this recent comment shows – "just a quick line to say a big THANK YOU for a wonderful day on Sunday. Your love for food shone through - all day long"

Holly and David source ingredients from

local experts such as Mark Lobb, Dartmouth fishmonger, who gets the fish for their hugely popular fish courses from Brixham fish market; meat comes from Jilly Rowden, Gara Barton and Sally Vincent; veggies come from Riverford and organic eggs from Edward Jones' flock at Fountain Violet Farm in Kingswear.

In May 2011 Manna from Devon celebrated their 5th birthday and to mark it Holly and David have put together a celebration Spring menu for Dartmouth Caring.

You can find out more information about Manna from Devon on their website: www.mannafromdevon.com

METHOD

A proper Minestrone is a wonderful thing full of briefly cooked vegetables and herbs with lots of fresh flavours. The vegetables used are infinitely variable depending on the seasons so you can vary the recipe throughout the year. Heat the oil in a saucepan and cook the shallot and garlic until soft but not coloured. Add half of the vegetables, season well and cook with the stock for 20 minutes. Add the rest of the vegetables and cook for 5 minutes giving a mix. Roughly chop the herbs and off the heat, stir in to the soup with the crème fraiche. Whizz briefly with a hand blender so the soup is half chunky. Serve hot or at room temperature with the cheese sprinkled over the top and some good bread.

INGREDIENTS - serves 6

1. 2 shallots, peeled and finely chopped
2. 2 tbsp olive oil
3. 8 stalks English asparagus, trimmed and cut into 1cm pieces
4. 2 handfuls fresh spinach, washed and shredded
5. 225g purple sprouting broccoli, trimmed and shredded
6. A handful of baby broad beans or garden peas.
7. 1 handful chard or spring greens, washed and shredded
8. 800ml chicken or vegetable stock
9. 2 tbsp crème fraiche
10. Small bunch fresh wild garlic
11. Small bunch fresh mint
12. 50g grated Sharpham Rustic cheese
13. Salt and pepper

INGREDIENTS - serves 6

1. 5cm thick t-bone steak weighing about 1.5kg.

2. Salt and freshly ground black pepper

3. 3-4 handfuls rocket and/or watercress

4. 2 tbsp extra virgin olive oil

5. Juice and zest 1 lemon

METHOD

This is a great recipe for a celebration – fantastic ingredients treated simply and served to friends. In Florence this cut would only be made from the local white cattle called Chiannina, however we always get a piece of South Devon beef from a good butcher or farmer. This sounds like a massive piece of meat but one steak will happily feed 6 people.

Heat the barbeque. Season the steak well.

Place the steak directly on to the grill. Cook for 10 minutes, until the steak is charred on one side and can easily be removed from the coals.

Cook for another 5-10 minutes on the second side for rare. Remove from the heat and rest for 5 minutes – the meat, not you...

Toss the rocket or watercress with the olive oil, lemon juice and zest and season well with salt and pepper. Carve the steak thinly and serve with the green salad and a bottle of Chianti.

METHOD

This is a delicious end to a meal – creamy fragrant rice with fresh, local rhubarb. It is nothing like the rice pudding of school day memories so do give it a try – it's a hugely popular end to our Eastern Mediterranean cooking days when we lunch on the deck in the sun overlooking the river. It looks stunning if you serve it in individual glasses with the bright pink fruit on top of the rice. Another flexible recipe as you can change the fruit to use peaches, apricots, plums as the year progresses.

Put the water, milk, cream, cardamom and rice into a pan. Bring to the boil and simmer gently until the rice is tender and the liquids nearly absorbed but still creamy.

Towards the end of cooking add the caster sugar to taste and stir to dissolve. Discard the cardamom pods, stir in the rosewater, turn into a serving dish or individual glasses and cool.

Put the rhubarb, sugar to taste, orange zest and juice and a little water into a pan. Simmer gently until the rhubarb is tender.

Cool, add to the top of the rice & serve.

INGREDIENTS - serves 6

1. 150g pudding rice
2. 350ml water
3. 350ml Devon double cream
4. 650ml milk
5. 3 cardamom pods
6. 2 tbsp rose water
7. 3-4 sticks young rhubarb, chopped into 3cm pieces
8. Juice and zest 1 orange
9. Sugar to taste

27 Lower Street, Dartmouth, Devon, TQ6 9AN. TEL: 01803 839278

CHEF NIGEL WAY

Nigel Way, who was awarded an MBE in 2009 for services to the community, has been at the heart of Dartmouth's tourist trade for more than a quarter of a century. Bringing his customary energy and enthusiasm for food and good times to the Royal Castle in the 1980s he and his wife Anne have now also started the Bayards Cove Restaurant.

He adds ' just to say I am a Westcountry boy and so were both my parents, originally living in and around Sidmouth in east Devon. I was educated at South Devon College and worked in London and Broadway, Worcestershire before coming back to Devon. The family is now firmly entrenched in Dartmouth. Both my children also love living in Devon and won't live anywhere else.

Nigel has contributed a recipe from his grandmother for Scotch Eggs and is delighted that Sheila Isaacs-Berry from the Captain's House has added a recipe from HER grandmother for Piccalilli! The feast is one all can savour...

METHOD

Sweat all vegetables except nettles, slowly in olive oil. Cover with 1/2 litre of vegetable stock and bring to the boil. Remove any scum that forms on the top. Season with salt and pepper and simmer for 5 minutes. Add the nettles and simmer for a further 3 minutes. Allow to cool slightly, then blitz in a food processor and pass through a sieve. Serve hot or cold topped with crème fraiche or quark

INGREDIENTS - serves 6

1. 15 asparagus stems chopped cook in water and cover for 5 minutes, use tips for garnish at the end. Use water and stems as stock and for rest of soup.

2. 2 sticks of celery chopped

3. 2 leeks (green part only) washed to remove the grit then finely slice

4. 50g celeriac peeled and diced

5. 3 cloves of garlic finely chopped

6. 55g nettles (wear kitchen gloves) washed

7. 1 litre of vegetable stock

8. 1 tbs of olive oil

Mr W's Scotch eggs

I remember Christmas Eve at my grandfather's house when I was required with my cousins to spend the afternoon around the kitchen table making Scotch eggs. It took from lunch time till after the radio was done playing Nine Lessons and Carols service from King's College Cambridge. With hindsight we children were detailed to making Scotch eggs to keep us out of mischief while my mum and my aunties were busy preparing for Christmas Day dinner. Make no mistake they are as my mum would have said "a real fuss and palaver to make but very yummy."

INGREDIENTS - serves 6

1. A couple of pounds of good sausage meat

2. Some spring onions

3. Apples and if required 2 cloves of garlic

4. 9 good sized free-range eggs

METHOD

Boil eight eggs, not much more than four minutes so they are soft in the middle. Run them under cold water as soon as possible, then crunch and peel. Meanwhile chop anything like onions, spring onions or garlic or possibly apple and mix with the sausage meat, add a good dollop of salt and pepper. Divide the sausage meat into eight even size balls. Get a baking tray ready, to store finished items prior to cooking. Bowl of seasoned flour. Get ready a bowl for homemade breadcrumbs (stale bread) blitzed in a food processor. One egg to eggwash – egg whipped with some water. Now the fun starts. You may want an extra pair of hands to help. I spread the sausage mix on one hand, pop the hardboiled egg on top of the sausage mix and draw the sausage mix up and around the egg, so no white is showing. Sounds easy! Fill any holes with additional sausage mix, press until this is even, all around the egg. Roll the egg in the flour then in the egg wash, then in the breadcrumbs. Finally put on the baking tray ready to fry. By now you will have sausage meat, flour and egg wash everywhere. Repeat with the other seven eggs. Heat some oil in a pan and deep fry until golden brown. Cool and eat. I now make Scotch eggs for summer picnics but they are great for anytime of the year. I guess the grownups used to eat our Scotch egg on Christmas Eve night!

Sheila Isaacs-Berry of The Captain's House - Grandma's Mustard Pickle

My grandparents Grace and William were proud parents of 9 children; they filled their home with love, laughter, and plenty of food.

I have fond memories of family dinners at my grandma's, with numerous aunts, uncles, cousins, my parents and sister, all sitting elbow to elbow at the table, our plates piled high with food. Vegetables, with plenty of salt and a pinch of bicarb, boiled to within an inch of their life, very well roasted meats and beef dripping gravy, home made horseradish sauce, so hot it made your eyes water! Not to mention the lovely puddings. Everything tasted wonderful.

I am delighted to share this recipe by my Darling Grandma Grace. I hope you like it as much as I do, and wish you happy pickling.

METHOD

Divide cauliflower into small sprigs; peel onions, cut marrow into small pieces (after removing middle, which is waste). Spread on dish and sprinkle with salt, 25g to every 250g of veg. Leave until next day and then drain well.

Mix turmeric, mustard, sugar with vinegar in a pan, then add veg, and spices (tied with muslin bag). Boil gently for 10 minutes. Mix the flour with a little vinegar and add to mix, stir constantly while it boils for a further 5 minutes.

Remove the bag of spice, and bottle.

INGREDIENTS

1. Medium cauliflower
2. 450g small pickling onions
3. Small marrow or gherkins if liked
4. 1 cucumber
5. 1.2 litres of white vinegar
6. 1 tbsp corn flour or plain flour
7. 25g mixed spice
8. 25g dry mustard
9. 25g turmeric
10. 25g caster sugar

METHOD

Another dish of my mother's, she was adamant that it could only be made with unpasteurised milk (not true) see below.

Heat milk to 70-80°C

Stir in rennet

Stir in honey (my preference)

Pour into serving bowls (individual or one big one)

Set aside in a cool room (not the fridge)

Should set in 2 hours you can then serve it or keep it in the fridge.

Served with grated nutmeg or fresh soft or stewed fruits and a girt dollop of clotted cream!!!

How it works

My mum's maiden aunt used to farm in Axmouth (East Devon) and take milk fresh from the cow hence the 70-80 degrees (blood heat)

Just stir in the honey and the rennet, (an enzyme from the fourth stomach of any young ruminates usually of cows) which acts as a setting agent, and helps the calves digest the mother's milk. (I remember Miss Broom making her own rennet – don't ask!

Stones Rennet Stores was an abbatoir based in Exeter when I was a boy. They used to make Stones glue, cow gum and furniture polish as well as rennet.

INGREDIENTS - serves 6

1. 2 pints milk (full fat)

2. 2 tsp rennet (Stones rennet made in Exeter is best)

3. 1 tbsp of caster sugar or honey

4. Optional: nutmeg, cinnamon,

5. Brandy or rum (never used by my mum)

6. Clotted cream a definite

STOKE LODGE HOTEL RESTAURANT

Stoke Fleming, Nr. Dartmouth, South Devon, TQ6 0RA TEL: 01803 770523

CHEF PAUL HOWARD

Stoke Lodge is a family-owned business, run by Christine and Steven Mayer - and it has built a reputation for fantastic customer service.

The challenges of running a hotel day to day also bring challenges for the kitchen staff – if people stay for a week, they want to be given a choice of food, so the menus are constantly changing.

This seemingly daunting prospect is no problem for Paul Howard and his team.

Paul, learnt his trade at St Helen's College on Merseyside. He worked in Liverpool for more than three years until a seemingly dream job offer completely changed his life.

Moving to Jersey, he took up a position at a hotel where he met his future wife Alison – and found happiness.

After a number of years the couple moved to the Lake District for two years, but found they and their two children missed the sea.

2007 saw them move to Devon when Paul took up his position at Stoke Lodge.

"I've always believed that you need to let the natural flavours of the food come through," he said. "People often overpower food with over flavouring, so I use the best ingredients and light sauces, letting the natural flavours come out.

"I'm not someone who touts their 'signature dish' because I think you should make sure ALL your dishes are your signature! You just need to make sure you are happy to send out every single thing you cook.

"I'm happy at Stoke Lodge because we have a great atmosphere in the kitchen, and all of us love to see happy customers! Chris and Steve set the tone for the place - they are professional and trust you to do your best and do well – we all respond to that."

METHOD

250g Arborio rice, slowly fried with 2 finely chopped shallots & olive oil. Add 1/4 pint if fish stock until absorbed. Add 1/4 medium finely diced baked squash (roasted in olive oil), finely grated parmesan, 1/8 pint double cream, chopped parsley & white wine, stir until desired texture is achieved. Just before serving add hand-picked white Brixham crabmeat, lemon juice and serve with Parmesan curls.

Parmesan Curls

Very finely grated Parmesan shaped into curls, non stick paper, add little olive oil, bake in hot oven for 10 minutes and leave to cool.

INGREDIENTS - serves 4

1. Olive oil
2. 2 shallots
3. 250g Arborio rice
4. 140ml of fish stock
5. 1 medium squash - finely diced and roasted in olive oil
6. 70ml of double cream
7. 85ml of white wine to taste
8. Chopped parsley
9. 1 tspn of lemon juice
10. 300g white hand-picked Brixham crabmeat
11. Grated Parmesan

INGREDIENTS - serves 4

1. 4 sea bass fillets
2. 4 courgettes
3. 32 green beans

Pepper Beurre Blanc

4. 2 sliced skinless red peppers
5. 2 chopped shallots
6. 285ml double cream
7. 250ml dessert wine
8. Quality fish stock
9. 115g hard butter cut into squares

METHOD

I prefer to lightly flour & sear the fish skin side down in olive oil and a little butter for 2 - 3 minutes each side.

In the same pan, add sliced courgettes and green beans, sauté until wilted, drain on kitchen paper, with fish fillets.

Pepper Beurre Blanc

Simmer peppers and shallots in pan with cream until reduced. Add wine and fish stock, bring to boil then thicken with butter until a glaze achieved.

To serve: drain and plate greens and place fish on top, pour Beurre Blanc around fish and garnish with finely chopped chives.

METHOD

Make pastry and bake blind.

Boil double cream & milk together and pour over 310g dark chocolate chopped small.

Whisk in eggs and pour into pastry case.

Bake at 160ºc, gas 3 for 20 minutes

INGREDIENTS - serves 4-6

1. 255g plain flour
2. 85g caster sugar
3. 170g margarine
4. Pinch salt
5. Half a beaten egg
6. Water to bind
7. 285ml double cream
8. 140ml milk
9. 310g dark chocolate
10. 1 1/2 eggs

DARTMOUTH ACADEMY

Science
Food Techn

Milton Lane, Dartmouth, Devon, TQ6 9HW. TEL 01803 839700

DARTMOUTH ACADEMY STUDENTS

Open since September 2010, Dartmouth Academy is one of a small number of schools nationally which offers education for learners of all ages. Academies are the fastest improving schools in England and some of the highest performing, and Dartmouth Academy is continuing this trend and is exceeding expectations, according to independent inspectors.

The Academy offers an 'outstanding' standard of teaching to learners aged 3-18. With a radical curriculum, a personalised approach to learning through distinct stages of teaching and a positive ethos that promotes excellence and achievement, the Academy adheres to three clear values - to care, to inspire and to excel.

Helen Buckland, Teacher of Food Technology and Maths said: 'We really try to challenge students with their cooking at the Academy, and encourage them to try different recipes. The main aim is to make them confident and able cooks!

'We have entered students for lots of competitions over the last few years, and have been successful in beating other schools and colleges in the South Hams.

'All the recipes we have included in our menu have been cooked by the students and their can-do attitude is vital in their success!

'We hold regular 'Community Lunches' to which we invite people from our community we think would be interested in seeing our facilities and enjoy a lunch cooked by the students.

The students prepare, cook and serve the meal. I think this gives them the boost of seeing how well received their cooking is, but also prepares them for being polite and professional when dealing with people. They also can see how enjoyable it can be to cook for people and be satisfied with a well prepared and served dish.'

STARTER - SMOKED MACKEREL PATE

METHOD

Skin the mackerel fillets and place in a blender with the other ingredients. Blitz for one minute.

Pile into individual ramekin dishes, garnish with lemon wedges and black pepper and serve with toast triangles or melba toast.

INGREDIENTS - serves 4

1. 4 - 5 smoked mackerel fillets
2. 300g cream cheese
3. Juice of 1 lemon
4. 1 tsp of horseradish sauce or cream.

INGREDIENTS - serves 4

1. Olive oil

2. 4 chicken legs

3. 4 rashers of thick cut smoked back bacon, chopped into lardons

4. 1 onion, halved and sliced

5. 1 tbsp of plain flour

6. 450ml of dry cider

7. 1 heaped tsp Dijon mustard

8. 1 small Savoy cabbage

9. 25g butter

METHOD

Heat the oven to 190°C, gas mark 5.

Fry the seasoned chicken legs in some olive oil for 3-4 minutes each side until browned.

Remove from the pan, and fry the bacon and onion for 3-4 minutes until golden.

Stir in the flour and cook for 1 minute, then gradually add the cider, stirring all the time.

Simmer for 2 minutes then add the mustard.

Put the chicken legs into a roasting tin; add the bacon and onion mixture from the frying pan, cover with foil and bake for 45 minutes until the chicken is cooked through. Check seasoning.

Steam the cabbage until tender add butter and serve with the chicken, adding some boiled new potatoes if you wish.

METHOD

Remove seeds from vanilla pod, place in a bowl
with the sugar and mix well. Add the butter and
cream together. Add the flour and a pinch of salt,
mix to a soft dough. Wrap in cling film and chill
in the fridge for 1 hour. Preheat oven to 160°C/
gas mark 3. Roll out the dough on a lightly floured
surface to 5mm thick. Using an 8cm cutter cut out
16 biscuits. Place on a greased baking sheet, bake
for 15 minutes until pale golden. Put on a cooling
rack to cool. Whip cream until thick. When the
shortbread is cool, assemble the biscuits into four
towers, placing whipped cream and raspberries
between each layer.

INGREDIENTS - serves 4

1. 1 vanilla pod, halved lengthways
2. 100g caster sugar
3. 200g unsalted butter, softened, plus extra
    for greasing
4. 300g plain flour
5. Pinch of salt
6. 2 boxes of raspberries
7. 500ml double cream

DARTMOUTH APPRENTICE

St Barnabas Church, Newcomen Road, Dartmouth, Devon TQ6 9BN. TEL 01803 83782C

CHEF ADAM PARNHAM

Dartmouth Apprentice is Devon's only training restaurant for the long-term unemployed – giving those who have been overlooked by society a second chance to build a career.

Taking apprentices on six-month contracts, the Dartmouth Apprentice trains each in either front of house or kitchen skills whilst putting them through an NVQ Level Two and giving them life skills workshops in CV development, communication skills, interview techniques and attitudes to work.

Adam Parnham, head chef at the restaurant, which is housed in the converted church of St Barnabas on the way to Dartmouth Castle overlooking the harbour, is widely experienced.

Adam has always had a passion for cooking, his inspiration coming from his grandmother and grandfather who were always creating pastries and breads.

For 10 years he travelled around the UK working in various successful establishments alongside some of the country's best chefs - Marco Pierre

ADAM PARNHAM

White, Jean Christophe Novelli and Keith Floyd.

Adam returned to Devon in 2008 inspired by his belief that it is without doubt the best part of the country for good quality local ingredients. He appreciates the supply of free ranging animals, English cheeses and the freshest fish right on the doorstep. Adam's menu has also been influenced by his time spent in the Abruzzo region of Italy.

He enjoys the added responsibility of being involved in a training restaurant that helps disadvantaged people get back into work and achieve NVQ qualifications. He describes his role as one of his biggest challenges so far, and one of the most rewarding.

STARTER - BEEF CARPACCIO WITH BEETROOT AND HORSERADISH

METHOD

Using a sharp knife, slice the beef very thinly (about 1/2cm thick) and place carefully between 2 pieces of greaseproof paper. Roll the beef fillet with a rolling pin to make it even thinner. Place the beef on a plate and cover with a piece of greaseproof paper. Set aside. Repeat for 3 more plates. Remove the beetroot leaves from the beetroot and set the leaves aside. Simmer the beetroot in a pan of boiling, salted water for 20-30 minutes, or until the skin eases away when pushed with your thumbs. Drain.

Finely grate the horseradish into a bowl and add the red wine vinegar, crème fraîche and salt and pepper, to taste. Mix well, taste and add more horseradish, salt or pepper if necessary. Set aside.

Blanch the reserved leaves in a pan of boiling water for about 30 seconds, drain and then toss in a bowl with oil, lemon juice, salt and pepper, to taste.

To serve, remove the greaseproof paper from the carpaccio. Drizzle over a little olive oil and lemon juice, to taste, and scatter the dressed beetroot leaves over the carpaccio. Peel the beetroot pieces and slice in half. Place the beetroot on top and dress with more olive oil, lemon, salt and pepper. Serve with the creamed horseradish

INGREDIENTS - serves 4

1. 250g beef fillet

2. Olive oil, to taste

3. 1 tbsp chopped thyme, leaves

4. 2-3 small beetroot, with their leaves, cut into quarters

5. 75g fresh horseradish, peeled

6. 1 tsp red wine vinegar

7. 150g creme fraiche

8. Lemon juice, to taste

INGREDIENTS - serves 4

Crab Ravioli

1. 250g white crab meat (shredded)
2. 2 garlic cloves, finely chopped
3. 3 spring onions, finely chopped
4. 250g ricotta
5. 3 tbsp grated parmesan
6. 3 tbsp dill
7. Generous pinch paprika
8. 1/2 tsp ground ginger
9. Juice and zest of 1/4 lemon
10. Cornish sea salt and freshly ground black pepper

Lemon and Parsley Butter

1. 200g butter
2. 1 lemon
3. Hand full of parsley

Pasta Dough

1. 500g pasta flour
2. 5 free range eggs
3. 2 egg yolks

METHOD

Place the flour in a food processor with the egg and egg yolk and keep whizzing until the mixture resembles fine but sticky breadcrumbs. Add a little water as necessary.

Tip the dough out onto a clean work surface and knead into a ball. Continue to knead for 1 minute; the dough should be quite stiff. Wrap in cling film and leave to rest in a cool place for 1 hour before rolling out.

Cut the dough into 2 pieces. Flatten each piece with a rolling pin and roll out to a thickness of about 5mm.

Fold over the dough. Set a pasta machine to its widest setting and pass the dough through the machine 7 times, refolding after each pass. The dough should form a rectangular shape about 7.5 x 18cm in size. It is important to work the dough until smooth and shiny, as this gives it the 'al dente' texture when cooked.

Repeat with the second piece of dough.

To roll out the pasta, set the rollers on the pasta machine to their widest setting. Pass the dough through the rollers. Do not fold the dough.

Repeat this process, decreasing the roller setting a notch at a time with each pass.

This should give you two nice pasta strips, make sure you flour the table well as they may stick.

For the filling, simply put all the ingredients into a bowl and work together, season to taste.

Spoon the filling out onto the sheet, leaving a 3 inch gap between each one.

Then brush the pasta with water to help them stick, lay the other pasta sheet over the top and press around each filling using the bottom of your hands; it's important that you remove the air bubbles or they will burst.

Then simply cut the pasta in-between each filling, you should make 12 raviolis.

Have a pan of boiling salted water at the ready.

Now melt the butter on a low heat in a pan big enough to hold the ravioli portions. Add the lemon juice and chopped parsley. Drop the ravioli into the water and cook until they float to the top; no longer as you want the pasta to be al dente.

Transfer the ravioli into the butter, serve straight away.

METHOD

Pour the cream into a thick bottomed saucepan, split the vanilla pod and add to it, and shred the mint leaves into the mix, bring to just under the boil. Whisk the eggs and sugar together then pour the cream in a little at a time and keep whisking or the mix may scramble the eggs. Then add the Pimms and pass the mix through a fine sieve. Quarter the strawberries into your moulds, and then divide the liquid mix between them. Place the moulds into an oven dish then half fill with water, place them in the oven at 140ºC/gas 1 for 35 minutes, then refrigerate before serving.

Brulée for top, sprinkle with demerara sugar and use cooking flame torch or lightly grill.

For the shortbread

Place the ingredients into a bowl and work together until it forms a dough, roll out and cut into desired shapes, place on baking paper and cook at 180ºC/gas 4 for 15 minutes. When you remove them from the oven, sprinkle with caster sugar and leave to cool on a rack.

INGREDIENTS - serves 4

1. 900ml double cream
2. 6 egg yolks
3. 1 egg
4. 1 vanilla pod
5. 150g caster sugar
6. 100ml Pimms
7. Hand full of fresh mint
8. 1 punnet of local strawberries

For the shortbread

1. 250g local butter
2. 250g plain flour
3. 70g caster sugar

THE SEAHORSE RESTAURANT

5 South Embankment, Dartmouth, Devon, TQ6 9BH. TEL: 01803 835147

CHEFS MITCH TONKS AND MAT PROWSE

Mitch Tonks is a highly acclaimed award winning restauranteur, food writer and fishmonger. Mitch, along with business partner and head chef Mat Prowse co-owns three restaurants – The Seahorse and The Rockfish Seafood and Chips restaurants and the Rockfish Grill & Seafood Market in Bristol. Mitch co-presented the TV series Mitch and Matt's Big Fish and writes regularly for magazines and newspapers, including Great British Food and Devon Life. He is also consultant chef for the boutique hotel South Sands in Salcombe. He also works closely with Visit South Devon and is leading their campaign promoting South Devon crab.

STARTER - POTTED SOUTH DEVON CRAB

METHOD

Melt the butter, stir in the crabmeat, cognac, the fennel, lemon juice and zest, chilli and season and taste and then put into ramekins and pour a little melted butter over the top then sprinkle with fennel fronds, chill well and serve with toast.

INGREDIENTS - serves 4

1. 250g brown meat
2. 150g white meat
3. Splash of cognac
4. 1 tsp ground fennel seeds
5. 1 crumbled dried chilli
6. 100g melted butter
   + 50g for pouring on top
7. Fennel fronds
8. Juice & zest 1/2 lemon

INGREDIENTS - SERVES 4

1. 8 Dover (or 'slip') soles about 250g
2. 2 beaten eggs
3. 150g plain flour
4. A couple of handfuls of really fine breadcrumbs
5. Enough vegetable oil for deep frying

For the tartare sauce

6. 2 egg yolks
7. 1 tsp Dijon mustard
8. Splash of white wine vinegar
9. 300ml vegetable oil
10. Squeeze of lemon
11. 1 shallot very finely chopped
12. 1 tbsp finely chopped tarragon
13. 2 gherkins finely chopped
14. 2 tbsp finely chopped capers
15. Salt and pepper

METHOD

First make the tartare sauce. Whisk together the egg yolks, mustard and vinegar and whilst whisking pour in the oil in a steady stream until you have a thick creamy mayonnaise. Taste and season and add a squeeze of lemon. Then stir in the shallot, tarragon, gherkins and capers. The sauce should be quite piquant and chunky and have the consistency of very thick double cream.

Prepare the soles for deep frying by having in front of you a bowl of the beaten egg, a plate for the flour and a plate for the breadcrumbs. First dip the fish in flour making sure it is well coated, then into egg and lastly in breadcrumbs making sure the fish have a nice even coating. Heat your oil to about 180°C and gently place the fish into the oil, 2 at a time. If you try to do too many at once the temperature of the oil will fall and your fish will not be crisp. After 4-5 minutes the fish should be a lovely golden colour, remove and drain on kitchen paper.

When all the fish are cooked place 2 fish, side by side on each plate, place a tablespoon of tartare sauce by the side, put a wedge of lemon on each plate as fish cooked in this way is delicious with lemon juice.

METHOD

Soak the gelatine leaves for 5 minutes in cold water and then drain well. Warm the syrup and add the gelatine, stir until dissolved but be careful not to boil. Add the remaining ingredients and stir well. Pour into 150 ml moulds or glasses and chill for a few hours or overnight until set.

INGREDIENTS - serves 4

1. 375ml Prosecco
2. 125ml sugar syrup (100g sugar dissolved in 100ml water)
3. 125ml Campari
4. 125ml orange juice
5. 7 leaves gelatine

SPICE BAZAAR RESTAURANT

St Saviour's Square, Church Close, Dartmouth, Devon TQ6 9DJ. TEL: 01803 832285

CHEF SHAHAR LASHKOR

Spice Bazaar, Dartmouth opened in St. Saviour's Square in December 2000 offering a unique, contemporary style of Indian Dining.

It is the perfect setting for curry lovers to indulge themselves in a funky fusion of design, innovation and exotic eastern cuisine.

Its ethos consists of using only the finest produce available and if possible locally produced ingredients -incorporating the delicate flavor of Asian spices to create a new, refreshing approach to Indian Cuisine with fantastic service too.

Shahar Lashkor, its founder and the Executive Chef, was born in Bangladesh and educated in Exeter. His first job experience at the Rouge Mont Hotel, in Exeter fired his imagination and offered the venue for the birth of his idea of "Fusion Cooking ".

His vision to create a restaurant depicting the merging of the East and the West became a reality in 2000 with the opening of Spice Bazaar – and it quickly established a reputation for high standards and a welcome to rival any restaurant in the land.

Shahar has both been a chef and a member of the local community, taking part in numerous Dartmouth Shakespeare Weeks and donating prizes, time and money to charity, including Dartmouth Caring.

Spice Bazaar won the 'Best Asian Restaurant in the South West' in 2008 and 2009.

Shahar said: 'I love cooking, bringing together different influences which compliment each other, using the best, usually locally sourced, ingredients. Dartmouth is a special town with many beautiful restaurants, but I think we manage to succeed because we serve fantastic food with great service and an inviting atmosphere.

'Dartmouth Caring is the perfect charity to support because it helps people in this community every single day of the year. I'm proud to have helped and delighted to continue my support for it.'

STARTER - ALOO AUR GOBI SALAD

METHOD

Add everything except four of the potatoes cauliflower and mooli to a food processor or blender and blend until you get a thick, smooth paste. Add the cauliflower, mooli & potatoes and put them in a bowl. Toss them with the sauce and serve chilled.

INGREDIENTS - serves 4

1. 1 small cauliflower cut in to small florets steamed but crunchy
2. 1 medium Indian mooli thinly cut (white radish)
3. 1 chopped fresh tomato
4. 4 1/2 chopped, medium sized cooked potatoes
5. 1/2 tablespoon sugar
6. 2 tsp dry mango powder
7. 1/4 tsp black pepper
8. 2 tbsp water
9. 1/2 tsp roasted ground cumin
10. 3 tbsp plain yogurt
11. 3 green chillies, halved & seeded
12. 2 tsp lemon juice or lime juice
13. Salt, to taste
14. 1 cup chopped coriander

INGREDIENTS - serves 4

1. 1 x 800- 1000g poussin or small chicken

For the marinade

1. Green paste
2. 225g fresh ginger
3. 175g fresh garlic
4. Good hand full of fresh coriander
5. 3/4 cup of white vinegar
6. 1 tbsp of olive oil
7. Good hand full of coriander and basil
8. 3 tbsp of mustard oil. If that's not possible olive oil.
9. 1 tbsp of cumin powder
10. 1 tbsp of coriander powder
11. 1/2 tbsp of Chilli powder
12. 1/2 tbsp of turmeric powder
13. 1 cup of greek yoghurt
14. Juice of 1 lime
15. 1 tbsp of salt
16. Olive oil for basting

METHOD

Skin and cut the poussin into four quarters making little slits in the breasts and leg.

Wash the cut poussin in slightly salted water leave for about 5 mins then remove from the water and leave it to drain in a colander.

First stage of the marinade

Combine the green paste, fresh ginger, fresh garlic, a good hand full of fresh coriander and 4 deseeded green chillis. To that, add 3/4 cup of white vinegar and 1 tbsp of olive oil and blend to a smooth paste. Pat dry the poussin and rub with the green paste, rub it well in to the bird and let it stand in the colander for atleast 10-15 mins.

Second stage of the marinade

In a bowl combine a good hand full of coriander and basil blended with as little water as possible, mustard oil, cumin powder, coriander powder, chilli powder, turmeric powder, greek yoghurt, juice of 1 lime and salt.

Add the poussin to the marinade mix and leave to stand for 2 hours covered by cling film.

You can either cook the poussin in the oven and finish off on the barbeque or do it all in the barbeque. Skewer the birds and cook over the flame turning and basting with olive oil for at least 10 to 12 min or till you are sure it is cooked.

Kofta Kebab

INGREDIENTS - serves 4

1. 500g lean minced lamb
2. 500g Boiled peeled potatoes
3. 5 garlic cloves
4. 1 large shallot
5. 2 tbsp of chopped mint
6. Dry rose petals
7. 2 tbsp of coarse semolina
8. Olive oil for basting
9. Corn flour for coating
10. Salt & pepper to taste

METHOD

Combine all the ingredients except the corn flour and olive oil in a food processor. Mix the lamb mince and potatoes to a fine smooth mix. Remove from the processor into a bowl. Make 8 balls and flatten to form a patte. Coat in corn flour and leave to rest till ready to grill on the barbecue for 3 minutes on each side.

METHOD

Place all the ingredients into a blender and mix well; serve in a long glass with a mint leaf on top. If desired adding a measure of Malibu will add a little twist. If adding Malibu, rose water can be discarded. Milk can be added to thin the lassi if necessary.

INGREDIENTS - serves 4

1. 3 cups of plain yogurt
2. 10 ice cubes, sugar to taste or if desired salt
3. 3 drops of rose water.
4. 1 cup (200ml) of milk
5. Few fresh mint leaves for decoration

DART MARINA HOTEL

Sandquay Road, Dartmouth, Devon, TQ6 9PH. TEL 01803 832580

CHEF TOM WOODS

Dart Marina was created using the old Sandquay workshops of the Philips and Son Boat builders in the 1960s and it has changed with the times to remain one of the most popular hotels in town.

Devon born and bred, family man Dart Marina head chef Tom Woods has more than 15 years experience in fine dining and banqueting, and his knowledge of local producers has been the result of living amongst them.

Tom said: "Devon is my home and I have been fortunate to grow up and work amongst beautiful landscape almost surrounded by the sea. I've lived in Salcombe for 15 years and have made some great friends amongst

local producers so I write my menus with the landscape, the sea and great producers in mind.

"To be made Head Chef was something I have worked hard to achieve. The restaurant is very well regarded and we are very proud here of the good reputation we have.

"I love bringing my own style to the menu with day-boat specials from Brixham and Plymouth and my own caught and smoked mackerel which I am just perfecting! Doing a menu for Dartmouth Caring is great, because it is such a well-regarded and fantastic charity. Anyone would support what they do, and if I can help with a menu, that's brilliant."

METHOD

Manuka Smoked Chicken Breasts are available from Mike's Smokehouse, in Loddiswell near Kingsbridge. This award winning, locally sourced, fresh West Country chicken breast is gently brined with honey and molasses, and then smoked with Manuka to a moist and tasty perfection. Manuka is a tea tree grown in New Zealand, offering a unique, light and delicate smoke flavour.

To make the dressing

Place the orange juice in a pan and reduce by approximately half, until slightly syrupy.

Then allow to cool and emulsify with about 2-3 tbsp of good olive oil. Then add the orange zest and finely chopped chervil.

To assemble the salad

Keep it rustic – simply mix all the ingredients together with the dressing, and serve in a bowl with some more dressing on the side – delicious!

INGREDIENTS - serves 4

1. 2 oranges – zest grated and blanched fruit and segmented
2. 1 bunch of watercress – washed and spun
3. 1 bunch of baby spinach – washed and spun
4. 1 small handful of walnuts
5. Olive oil
6. 1/2 ltr orange juice
7. A small bunch of chervil

INGREDIENTS - serves 4

The Pork

1. 2kg Pork Belly - boned, skin on, (I use Poole Farm pork)

Marinade

1. 100g caster sugar
2. 100g sea salt
3. 1 sprig of thyme
4. 1/2 bulb of garlic (peel the cloves first)
5. 5g white peppercorns
6. 5g coriander seeds
7. 5g star anise
8. 5g juniper berries
9. 2g cloves
10. 1 orange - peel and juice
11. 1 bay leaf
12. 50ml water

Salad

1. 2 oranges - peeled and finely sliced
2. Hand full of walnuts
3. Baby spinach
4. Watercress
5. 2 Pink Lady apples – leave the skin on but core the apple, cut into 8 segments, sprinkle with a light touch of Five Spice, then cook in the oven until slightly softened but still holding its shape. Toss together; just before serving, a little walnut oil is also nice added.

Sauce

1. 250 - 300ml stock
2. 50g honey
3. 3 star anis

For the sauce - we use veal stock which we reduce down with honey and infuse with star anise. You can buy fairly good ready-made veal stock or jus, then simply add the other ingredients and reduce to get a glossy, dressing-type of consistency.

METHOD

This may look like a complicated recipe, and indeed it does need forward thinking, however the integral parts are all quite simple and the results stunning.

One large piece of belly as a centre piece for everyone to share would be a great easy eating slow lunch or dinner.

It's worth reading through the recipe first and make sure you allow enough time for each stage – you could start the day before for instance! Put the radio on, make a coffee and enjoy the process – the results are worth the time cooking!

To cook the pork

Wash off the marinade, then place the pork in a fairly deep roasting tray and just cover with oil (sunflower, groundnut or light olive oil) - cook for 10 hrs at 90 degrees - yes 10 hours, this is a confit (from the French confire - to preserve!)

After 10 hours, take the pork out of the oil and place on a clean tray, under a weight - (tip - place a layer of non-stick paper on top of the pork then a metal tray on top with either weights or heavy cans/books on top!) leave weighted for two hours. The oil can be re-used either to confit another pork or for roasting potatoes.

To finish

Score the skin and place skin side down in a hot, non stick, oven proof pan on top of the stove, then into the oven to re-heat fully and to get a nice crispy skin. Approx 20 mins but check that the pork is completely hot and the skin crisped.

You can always finish under the grill to crisp the skin if needed – but don't take your eyes off it!!

Serve with the salad and sauce including the whole star anise.

METHOD

Prepare the shortbread base by creaming the butter and sugar. Then add the flour. Cover and chill for 20mins.

Roll out onto a flat sheet and bake at 180°C/gas 4 for about 15mins. Then allow to cool slightly. Cut into 4 inch portion size discs. You will need to have four cutters. Keep the cutters on the disc as this provides a shape for the tart filling mixture.

To prepare the filling mix

Melt together the butter and chocolate in a bowl over hot water. Remove. Then place the egg, egg yolks and sugar over the water and whisk till a ribbon stage. Mix the two together lightly while ensuring all is fully incorporated. Pour over the biscuit base still in the cutters and chill. To serve place a warm sharp knife around the edge of the tart and push out. I serve this with homemade mascarpone ice cream and orange syrup.

To prepare the orange syrup

Add all the ingredients together – dissolve sugar in the juice then boil to reduce by half to a thin syrup consistency, allow to cool.

INGREDIENTS - serves 4

Shortbread base

1. 375g butter
2. 185g caster sugar
3. 500g flour

Tart filling

1. 150g dark chocolate
2. 100g butter – unsalted
3. 1 egg
4. 2 egg yolks
5. 30g sugar

Orange syrup

1. 300ml orange juice
2. 1 shot Cointreau
3. 100g sugar

DART TO MOUTH DELI

Old Market, Market St, Dartmouth, Devon TQ6 9QE. TEL: 01803 839377

CHEF HELEN WATTS

Dart to Mouth is the archetypal friendly local business – people pop in for a chat before they get their home-cooked food, and come back time and again, becoming friends as well as customers.

Run by Helen Watts and her daughter Dannii, its small premises in Dartmouth's historic Old Market Square buzz all day with conversation, the sound of laughter and the intoxicating smell of good honest food being prepared in the best possible way.

"I believe in cooking with really good fresh ingredients – you are what you eat and the better the food you take in, the better, I believe, you will be," said Helen.

"I learnt to cook with my grandmother, Dinah, who had her own outside catering company – based on volunteering in Bristol and Gloucestershire."

"From the age of 8 I would go and help her in the kitchen helping her to cook all the lunches for the oldies at the clubs she provided for every day. I still use a number of her recipes to this day – Nannie's Fruitcake with Marmalade is still the best seller in the shop."

"Dinah gave me my philosophy - if you eat food that is full of chemicals it gets into your system. So throw away the margarine and get out the butter, that's my philosophy!"

"I chose Autumn because I love to get out into the hedgerows and the fields and find all the roots, mushrooms and the like which are all new and fresh then – and delicious. We've gone for comforting food for the time when the nights are drawing in, old fashioned and lovely."

"I shared food with my family – I was lucky enough to be raised in a small holding – it was like the Good Life! We had a cow, grew our own vegetables, made our own cheese, had geese, chickens, the whole thing. When you are surrounded by this, and your family it's amazing. I now work in an old market, cooking old fashioned and wholesome recipes, and I work with my daughter Dannii – I'm very very lucky!"

STARTER - MUSHROOM SOUP SERVED WITH GARLIC CROUTONS

METHOD

Finely chop onions garlic & celery sauté very gently in butter; this will take approx 1 hr (if the mixture cooks too quickly, add a little water from time to time to the process) they should be very soft and light in colour. Chop the mushrooms add to the pan turn up the heat and cook until no liquid remains – now add the brandy and cook off – now add the stock and milk, bring up to simmering now cool a little and blend with a stick blender, season to taste.

For the garlic croutons: any stale bread, fresh garlic, olive oil, fresh thyme, sea salt. Cut the bread into any format you desire - put in a baking tray sprinkle with oil, garlic, salt and thyme toss around in the tray and bake in med oven for approx 15 minutes.

INGREDIENTS - serves 4

1. 500g mixed mushrooms
2. 50g butter
3. 1 medium to large onion
4. 2 cloves garlic
5. 2 sticks celery
6. 2 sprigs fresh thyme or tarragon
7. 250ml veg stock
8. 250ml whole milk
9. 1 tbsp brandy
10. Salt and pepper to taste

INGREDIENTS - serves 4

1. 500g best topside Devon beef, cut into large dice.

2. 1 very large onion

3. 2 large carrots

4. 2 celery sticks

5. 1/2 medium swede

6. 2 bay leaves

7. Beef stock/cubes if you like

8. 1 tsp redcurrant jelly

METHOD

Chop all the veg, sauté in beef dripping if you have it. Pan fry the beef very hot so that it sears. Put all the fab flavoursome foods together in casserole, cover with the stock, cook for 2-3 hours, 160°C/gas 3, thicken and cook for 10 mins. Serve with good bread or buttered mash.

Thoughts!

You can add mushrooms any other roots, garlic, herbs, wine or beer. YOU can make this a family supper or gourmet dinner!

PUDDING - DEVON APPLE CAKE DRIZZLED WITH DEVON HONEY

METHOD

Cream butter and sugar (white and fluffy) add eggs flour and extract. Peel core and chop 1 apple and core the other; put the chopped apple into the mixture either put into a single lined tin or in paper lined bun ties. Now decorate the top with slices of apple. Bake at 150°C for approximately 30 minutes. Drizzle with honey immediately after cooking. Serve with Devon clotted cream.

INGREDIENTS - serves 4-6

1. 115g self raising flour
2. 115g butter
3. 115g caster sugar
4. 2 medium eggs
5. 2 sweet Devon apples
6. Vanilla extract (please don't use flavour)
7. Runny honey from Devon

KENDRICK'S RESTAURANT

29 Fairfax Place, Dartmouth, Devon TQ6 9AB. TEL: 01803 832328

CHEF TOM STEPHEN

Kendrick's Restaurant, under the ownership of Bob and Georgia Kendrick, is now in its 11th year of trading. It has always tried to provide an interesting and varied menu with blackboard specials which are regularly changed. It has gained a great reputation for the quality and freshness of its food most of which is sourced locally.

Opening 7 nights a week all year round, Kendrick's is renowned for its relaxed, yet vibrant atmosphere. The following recipes have been created by Tom Stephen, one of Kendrick's strong team of chefs. Tom has a varied background, having worked with renowned chefs around the South West, and training in pastry at South Devon College.

However, he found somewhere he could be happy and express himself when he came to work at Kendricks, and has not looked back in the years he has been there. He said that the reasons for this are very simple: Everyone gets on, and they cook food that their customers love.

He said: "It's nice to introduce people to things which they haven't tried – we try to simplify things, strip it back to the flavours we love. That simplicity attracts people.

'We have a small team at Kendrick's and we work very well together. We have to ensure that every time people visit us, no matter who is in the kitchen, the customer gets the same experience. I'm a trained pastry chef, but the brilliant thing about our small kitchen team is you have to do everything.

'I'm genuinely happy at Kendrick's because it feels like a family – everyone in the team feels part of something good and positive. We love welcoming everyone to our restaurant and making them feel special, and letting them eat fine food.'

STARTER - BUTTERNUT SQUASH AND GARLIC SOUP

METHOD

Combine butternut squash onion and garlic in olive oil and roast in oven for 30mins or until tender. Add vegetables to stock and bring to boil, blend and add seasoning and dash of cream.

INGREDIENTS - serves 4-6

1. 2lb peeled, sliced and diced butternut squash
2. 2 tblsp olive oil
3. 4 cloves garlic peeled and sliced
4. Pinch salt and pepper
5. 1 1/2 pints veg stock
6. 1 diced onion
7. Dash of double cream to finish

INGREDIENTS - serves 4-6

1. 2 medium sized pheasants
2. 8 rashers streaky bacon
3. 2 carrots, chopped
4. 2 sticks of celery, chopped
5. 2 onions, chopped
6. 2 gloves of garlic
7. Several sprigs of parsley
8. 50g dried cranberries
9. 1/2 pint port
10. 225g sausage meat
11. 70g breadcrumbs
12. 70g toasted pinenuts
13. 1 egg
14. 4 large jacket potatoes
15. 100g diced bacon
16. 1/2 Savoy cabbage, sliced
17. 1/4 pint red wine
18. 2 tbsp red currant jelly
19. Vegetable oil
20. 100g butter
21. Salt and black pepper

For the stuffing: Soak 50g dried cranberries in port for 1 hour. Fry 1/2 diced onion in butter add 1 chopped garlic clove then mix with 225 g sausage meat, 70g breadcrumbs and 70g toasted pinenuts, add cranberries and bind together with egg.

For the pheasant: Remove the legs and breasts from the pheasant. Season the legs with salt and freshly ground black pepper. Place in a casserole, cover with vegetable oil and cook on a low heat for 1 hour.

Butterfly the breast and fill with stuffing fold and wrap in streaky bacon, cling film and leave in fridge until ready to cook. Heat oil in pan until hot brown off breast on both sides then place in a preheated oven at 180°C/gas 4 cook for further 8mins. Remove and leave to rest for 5 mins.

For the jus: Sweat off an onion in oil until tender add 1/4 pint port and 1/4 pint red wine, reduce by half then add 1 pint of reserved stock, reduce again by half then add 2 tblspn red currant jelly and reduce until coats back of spoon.

Serve the breast, together with the leg confit, colcannon mash, seasonal vegetables and jus.

METHOD

For the colcannon mash: bake 4 large jacket potatoes, leave to cool slightly before scooping out the potato, then cook half onion and half the garlic in some butter add some diced bacon cook until crisp then add 1/2 sliced savoy cabbage cook until tender; leave to cool, combine with potato and check seasoning.

For the stock: put the pheasant carcass in a large saucepan with the carrot, celery, onion, garlic and parsley stalks. Cover with water, bring to the boil and simmer for 40 minutes.

Strain and return the liquid to the heat. Simmer until reduced by half. Reserve this stock to use in the sauce.

METHOD

Oven 180ºC/gas 4

Slice french stick in half lengthways and butter both sides and cut into cubes. Whisk whole eggs, yolk and sugar until creamy then whisk in cream and baileys then add dates.

Soak bread in egg mixture for half an hour. Cling 6/8 dariole moulds and fill with bread mix. Place in deep baking tray with water half way up moulds and cook for 30 -40 mins until golden. Leave to cool slightly then turn out and serve with toffee sauce, cream, icecream or custard.

INGREDIENTS - serves 6

1. 1/2 large French stick
2. 50g butter
3. 25g caster sugar
4. 60g dates chopped
5. 2 egg yolks
6. 2 whole eggs
7. 600ml double cream
8. 4 tbsp Baileys

THE LAUGHING MONK RESTAURANT

Totnes Rd, Strete, Devon, TQ6 0RN. TEL: 01803 770639

CHEF BEN HANDLEY

The Laughing Monk Restaurant was originally the village school dating back to 1839. The school was closed in the 1960s and subsequently turned into a restaurant. Ben and Jackie Handley now own The Laughing Monk having made the move from Derbyshire to Devon in March 2008. Both have a wealth of experience working in award winning Country House hotels and strive to bring that level of quality to their own restaurant.

The restaurant was sympathetically refurbished in January 2009 retaining many of the School's original features, including the original floor, doors and windows. It now has a light and airy feel for the summer and when the shutters are closed and the wood burner is lit a warm cosy evening can be enjoyed in the winter.

The Laughing Monk is now an award-winning restaurant with both an AA Rosette and Taste of the West "Gold" Award – both were awarded in November 2009.

"Food at the restaurant is all about simplicity and freshness with much of the produce coming from our door step," said Ben. "When the produce is this local and this good you really are spoilt for choice. This is why our menu changes regularly to take advantage of what's available and at its best.

"All our fish and seafood comes from Start Bay caught by local boats out of Dartmouth. These may include lobsters, crabs, seabass, lemon sole, skate and scallops. We love being here – we work hard and love giving good service and good food.

"Our Service is friendly, unobtrusive and efficient. We are a family-friendly restaurant and encourage families with small children to take advantage of our "Early Supper Menu" which runs from Monday-Saturday. 5pm-7pm in the summer and 6.30pm-7.30pm in the winter. Visit our website www.thelaughingmonk.com."

METHOD

First of all heat a sauce pan and melt the butter; fry off the garlic, onions, thyme and rosemary so that they are soft and have taken on a little colour, remove from the heat and allow to cool.

Butter a 12 inch Le Creuset dish terrine mould and line with cling film allowing plenty of excess for covering the top later. Next line the mould with the streaky bacon going from side to side making sure there are no gaps.

In a large bowl mix together the pork fat, chicken livers, (ask your butcher to mince these for you), eggs and cream, making sure there are no big lumps of pork fat. In the same bowl gently mix in by hand the remaining ingredients. Before you fill the terrine moulds with the mixture cook a little in a pan and then taste, check and adjust the seasoning if needed.

Once you're happy with the taste fill the mould right up to the top and then fold over the loose ends of the bacon so that all the mixture is covered. Next bring over the spare cling film and carefully cover the terrine so that everything is well sealed. Place the terrine in a deep oven tray and half fill with water, cook for 1 1/2 hours at 175°C/gas 3. Once the terrine is cooked remove from the tray and press in the fridge for 24 hours.

Serve with some homemade chutney and toast.

INGREDIENTS - serves 4-6

1. 250g streaky bacon
2. 250g minced pork fat
3. 250g minced chicken livers
4. 100g diced pheasant breast
5. 100g diced pigeon breast
6. 150g diced venison loin
7. 2 eggs
8. 50ml cream
9. 50g pitted prunes
10. 50g raisins
11. Zest of 1 orange
12. 2 cloves garlic (finely chopped)
13. 1 large onion (finely chopped)
14. 1/2 tsp dried thyme
15. 1/2 tsp chopped rosemary
16. Cracked black pepper
17. 50g butter

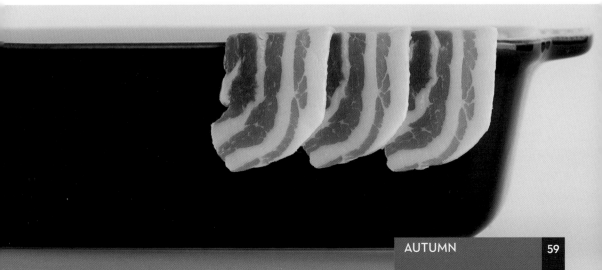

INGREDIENTS - serves 4-6

1. 120g beef cheeks (trimmed)
2. 1/2 bottle red wine
3. 1/2 bottle port
4. 1 onion
5. 2 carrots
6. 2 leeks
7. 1/2 head celery
8. 1/2 bulb garlic
9. 12 pepper corns
10. Bunch mixed herbs (rosemary, thyme and tarragon)
11. 1 ltr beef stock seasoning

METHOD

Trim the beef cheeks by removing any excess fat and sinew or ask your butcher to do it for you. Place the cheeks into a deep oven tray or large pan. Peel the onions, carrots, leeks and garlic and roughly chop; add to the beef cheeks along with the remaining ingredients. Cover with foil and put in the oven for 12 hours. Please note the oven should be on its lowest setting about 120ºC. When the cheeks are cooked they will feel very soft and tender. Put them into the fridge over night to chill; this will firm them up and make it easier to handle them. Once the cheeks have chilled remove them from the cooking stock, carve and put them into a clean pan or oven dish. Put the cooking stock into a saucepan and bring to the boil; thicken slightly with some beurre maniere pass through a fine sieve and pour onto the beef cheeks and check seasoning. Re-heat in the oven for 20-30 minutes. Serve with horseradish mash and buttered Savoy cabbage.

METHOD

Heat a large heavy based frying pan until very hot. Peel the bananas and cut in half length ways toss them in the 70g of sugar and then place them into the pan, allow to cook for 2 minutes on either side making sure the sugar is well caramelised. Remove from the pan and allow to cool. Once cooled place in the food processor with the Baileys and blend to a smooth paste. To make the Bavarois, separate the eggs and whisk the yolks with the sugar to ribbon stage. Meanwhile boil the milk and soak the gelatine in cold water. Pour the milk over the egg yolks and sugar mix together. Place in a bowl over ice to cool. Cook on a low heat until the custard coats the back of a wooden spoon. Add gelatine and stir to dissolve. Whilst the egg mix cools firstly whisk the cream to soft peaks and then in a separate bowl whisk the egg whites until they become stiff. Once the egg mix has cooled and is starting to set mix in the banana puree then carefully fold in the whipped cream and the whisked egg whites, check taste and add more Baileys if needed. Place into small moulds and set in fridge. To serve dip mould gently in hot water and turn out, serve with melted chocolate sauce.

INGREDIENTS - serves 4-6

1. 200ml milk
2. 200ml cream
3. 100g caster sugar
4. 6 egg yolks
5. 6 egg whites
6. 5 leaves gelatine
7. 4 large "ripe" bananas
8. 70g caster sugar
9. 2 large shots Baileys
10. 200ml cream
11. 150g dark chocolate melted

ANGELIQUE RESTAURANT

2 South Embankment, Dartmouth, Devon, TQ6 9BH. TEL 01803 839425

CHEF DARREN BROWN

Learning his trade at Botleigh Grange Hotel in Southampton - starting as a potwasher and working his way up over six years to Chef de Partie - Darren Brown has been a hard working and dedicated chef his whole career - but he knew where he wanted to be: the country.

"After a recommendation from a friend I left to work at the Lanesborough Hotel in Hyde Park, London, but I'm a country boy at heart and I just couldn't settle. I was living in Dulwich so it was a real shock to the system moving up from Hampshire.

"I went back to Botleigh Grange as sous chef for another five years. By the time I was 28 I was head chef and had two rosettes..

"I left for a position as junior sous chef at Monsieur Max in Hampton Hill. My senior sous chef was Tom Kerridge, who now owns the Hand & Flowers in Marlow. That was a big turning point for me as it was my first Michelin starred kitchen. It was a great experience to learn new ingredients, new techniques and things I've never seen before. It set me on my path really and gave me a base to grow from."

He then started his own restaurant with backers and gained a Michelin Star of his own. After seven years that restaurant was sold, and Darren was looking for a new challenge. His old senior sous chef came to the rescue:

"That was where my first contact with Alan Murchison came. Tom introduced me and we hit it off straight away. Now I've opened my latest venue in Dartmouth. I'm not a big city boy - I don't feel comfortable there. I'm enjoying my fishing and going for walks in the fresh air - you don't get to do that a lot in London."

"I love Dartmouth, and I'm not one to move around every couple of years. I can feel myself still being in Dartmouth, full to capacity every service and making people happy in years to come. "

STARTER - SCALLOPS, CAULIFLOWER, HAM

METHOD

Place ham between two sheets of grease proof paper and place on a flat tray. Place in a pre heated low oven at 60ºc until crispy (about 3 hours). Remove from oven and cool. Snap each slice into 3 pieces, and set aside.

Cut cauliflower into smallish pieces and put into boiling salted water. Cook until just soft, about 4-5 mins. Strain cauliflower and put back into the dry pan, add cream and bring to the boil. Remove from heat and place into a liquidiser. Blend until smooth. Add in the butter and blend on full speed for 2 minutes to ensure a smooth puree. Season with a little salt and ground white pepper.

Heat a heavy bottom pan, and add a little veg oil. When the oil is hot add the scallops to the pan one at a time placing them in a circle starting at 12 o'clock and working clockwise. When the 12 o'clock scallop is golden (Approx 1 minute), turn the scallops in the same order as you placed them in the pan. This is to ensure even cooking time. Cook for a further minute then remove pan from the heat. Add lemon juice to the pan, and add the butter. Coat the scallops with the liquor, using a spoon. Take the scallops from the pan and drain on a clean new cloth.

INGREDIENTS - serves 4

1. **12 washed and dried scallops (3 per portion)**

2. **250gs cauliflower**

3. **100g double cream**

4. **60g unsalted butter**

5. **1/2 lemon juiced**

6. **10g butter**

7. **4 slices Parma ham**

8. **Salt and pepper**

9. **Celery shoots**

INGREDIENTS - serves 4

1. 4 x 170g venison steaks, (topside from seamed out leg muscles)

2. 4 sticks of salsify

3. 1 Savoy cabbage

4. 1 x 200g pack of cooked chestnuts

5. 1 lemon juiced

6. 10g plain flour

7. 200ml beef stock

8. 80ml red wine

9. 200g butter

10. Salt and pepper

METHOD

Peel and wash the salsify cut into 2inch lengths and place each stick into a little water that has the lemon juice in it, just to stop the salsify turning brown. In a sauce pan, mix the flour with a little cold water to make a paste and add 1 pint of boiling water and a little salt. Add the salsify sticks and cook gently on the stove, taking care not to boil. Test the salsify with the tip of a small knife to see if it is just soft. About 10 mins. Remove from the heat and place the sticks of salsify on to a tray to cool.

Pick the outer leaves off the cabbage and cut out the centre stalks, and finely shred, with the heart of the cabbage. Cook the cabbage in boiling water untill it softens, remove from water and cool in ice water. Drain and dry.

Put 50gs of butter the stock and the red wine and place into a wide pan. Add the chestnuts and cook slowly so that the stock slowly reduces until it become a sauce consistency. Remove from the heat.

Pre heat an oven to 180°C/gas 4. Quickly sear the venison steaks in a hot frying pan with a little oil to colour all sides. Place on a small tray and cook in the oven for 8 minutes (Medium Rare). Take from oven and leave on the side covered with a little foil on top to rest for 10 mins.

To plate:

Heat the cabbage in a little water and drain, brush with a little melted butter, season and put into rings.

Heat a frying pan with a little oil and butter, fry the salsify sticks till golden.

Place cabbage in the middle of the plate, and place salsify sticks in a neat pile next to cabbage.

Slice the venison steaks and season with salt and pepper, fan out on top of cabbage. Warm up the chestnuts in sauce and spoon them on and around the venison.

METHOD

Poached Pears

In a pan big enough to hold the pears, add in all the ingredients except the pears. Bring to the boil. Simmer for 10 mins to infuse, drop in pears, cover and gently poach for about 25 - 30 mins until soft. Turn off the heat and set aside. When cool cut in half length ways and using a parisienne scoop or small tea spoon cut out the core. The pears can be poached up to 2 days ahead and kept in the poaching syrup in the fridge.

Frangipane Mix

Cream the butter and sugar. Beat in the eggs. Stir in ground almonds and sieved flour. Stir in lemon juice.

Line an 8in flan ring with sweet pastry and bake blind. Set aside. When cool spread a little apricot jam on the bottom of the cooked tart case. Spoon on the frangipane to just below the top, and smooth over with a palette knife. Place the pear halves in a circle on the frangipane and gently push them in a little.

Bake at 180°C/gas 4 for 20-25 mins until even golden colour. Test with a small knife as you would for a sponge cake. Remove from oven, and cool. Remove from ring. Heat a little more of the apricot jam with a little water and when smooth, brush over the top of the tart to glaze. Serve with the yoghurt ice cream.

Yoghurt Ice Cream

Boil milk powder, milk, sugar and cream and cool. Then when cool stir into the yoghurt. Pour into ice cream machine and churn and freeze.

INGREDIENTS - serves 4

Poached Pears

1. 400g golden caster sugar
2. 400g water
3. 1 cinnamon stick
4. 2 strips lemon zest (use a potato peeler)
5. 1 star anise
6. 1 vanilla pod, split lengthways
7. 2 cloves
8. 4 ripe pears, peeled

Frangipane Mix

1. 200g butter
2. 200g caster sugar
3. 4 eggs
4. 150g ground almonds
5. zest and juice of 2 lemons
   (boiled, reduced by half, and cooled)
6. 50g plain flour

Yoghurt Ice Cream

1. 500g natural yoghurt
2. 35g milk powder
3. 250g milk
4. 200g caster sugar
5. 50g double cream

ANNABELLE'S KITCHEN

24 South Embankment, Dartmouth, TQ6 9BB. TEL: 01803 833540

CHEF JOHN HODGSON

John and Jo Hodgson were quickly accepted after opening Annabelle's Kitchen on the South Embankment in Dartmouth during the summer of 2010. They have built a reputation of friendly service and high quality food within the restaurant's cosy and welcoming confines.

John was trained at the Tante Marie Kitchen School, famous for producing the world's best chefs since 1954. He has an extensive experience as a caterer of large-scale events and private parties and his unflappable and friendly demeanour give the impression of a man who

can handle any situation.

Jo, who looks after front of house at the restaurant, has a wide experience of event management and wedding planning, and knows how to look after customers in the best way possible.

Eat at their restaurant and you will be struck by its intimacy, their friendliness, the seasonality and high-quality of the menu, and the fact that both will bring food out to customers.

They pride themselves on using local producers

and the best ingredients they can – the quality of the food they provide reflects their love of top quality ingredients. Annabelle's Kitchen is their first restaurant and they are bringing zeal, energy and fun to what to many would be a daunting task. Their first full weekend in the restaurant was Regatta weekend, so they clearly love a challenge, and seem to barely break a sweat.

STARTER - PAN FRIED CHICKEN LIVERS WITH CARAMELISED APPLES ON WALNUT TOAST

METHOD

Fry the sliced apple with a knob of butter in a pan with a sprinkle of sugar until golden brown and tender. Set aside. Then fry the chopped bacon for a few minutes, then add a knob of butter and once melted add the chicken livers and fry for 2 minutes, making sure they don't overcook, they should only just be cooked through. Return the apples and the bacon to the pan halfway through cooking, and season with a sprinkle of salt. Remove all the ingredients from the pan and set aside.

Pour the cider vinegar into the hot pan to deglaze, using a wooden spoon to loosen any bits. Add a splash of rapeseed oil if necessary

Toast the bread and spread with salted butter.

To serve, place the livers on top of the toast with the apples, sprinkle with the bacon and toasted nuts, then drizzle over the juices and some thyme leaves. Garnish with the watercress and serve.

INGREDIENTS - serves 4

1. Red apples, cored but not peeled and sliced into eighths
2. 400g chicken livers, all white sinew removed
3. 100g smoked streaky bacon, chopped into small pieces
4. 4 knobs of salted butter
5. Handful of toasted hazelnuts
6. 1 tsp cider vinegar
7. Rapeseed oil
8. Fresh thyme
9. Walnut bread or similar
10. Watercress, to garnish

INGREDIENTS - serves 4

1. 400g venison mince – your butcher will be able to mince this for you, you can also use beef

2. 6 small red onions

3. 1 tbsp of mixed herbs (oregano, thyme, rosemary)

4. 1 egg, to bind

5. 1 tbsp seasoned breadcrumbs

6. 1 large white onion, finely chopped

7. 4 slices smoked streaky bacon

8. Rapeseed oil, for frying

9. 700g parsnips, peeled, cored and chopped

10. Salted butter

11. Double cream

12. 4 large leaves of curly kale

13. Large glass of red wine

14. Redcurrant jelly

15. 1 pint chicken stock

METHOD

Preheat the oven to 190°C/gas 4. Roast 4 of the small red onions in the oven with a sprinkle of thyme, until soft. Fry off the white onion with some oil and a sprinkle of salt, in a medium pan until soft and translucent. Set aside to cool in basin.

In a bowl mix together the cooked onion, herbs, breadcrumbs, egg and minced venison and season. Mix well and shape the venison mix firmly into sausage shapes and squeeze to remove any air bubbles.

Wrap a slice of bacon around each sausage, rest sausages in fridge and then fry off in a pan to brown all over. Transfer to an oven for approximately 12-15 minutes. Allow to rest for a few minutes before serving.

Place the parsnips in a large saucepan, cover with water, bring to the boil, and cook until tender. Blanche the curly kale in salted boiling water until tender and then drain. Mash the parsnips, add a knob of butter and some cream, and season.

To make the gravy, fry 2 finely sliced red onions in a frying pan with some butter until soft, and then add a glass of red wine. Allow the wine to reduce, and then stir in 2 heaped tbsp of redcurrant jelly. Add a pint of chicken stock, bring to the boil and cook until you reach the right consistency. You may need to add some cornflour. Season to taste.

Place some curly kale in the centre of a plate, add a large spoonful of the parsnip mash, place two sausages on top, scatter around the roasted onions and pour the gravy around the plate.

METHOD

To make the pastry, sift together the flour and sugar into a large mixing bowl. Work the butter into the flour with your fingers until it resembles fine breadcrumbs. Add the lemon zest and beaten eggs. Add enough iced water until the dough begins to hold together. Press the dough into a rough ball, transfer to a lightly floured surface, then flatten slightly with your hand to make a round. Wrap in clingfilm and place in the fridge for an hour. Preheat the oven to 180°C/gas 4, roll out the dough and place in a 12" tart case, and allow the sides to overhang a little. Prick the bottom with a fork, line with baking parchment and fill with baking beans. Bake until the crust is set and slightly browned, about 20 minutes. Reduce the oven to 170°C, remove the beans and baking paper and bake for another 10 minutes, until browned all over the base. This can be done in advance and allowed to cool. Melt the syrup and butter in a pan. Remove from the heat, and add the ginger, lemon juice, beaten egg and breadcrumbs. Pour into the tart case and cook for 20 minutes, or until firm to touch in the centre. Leave the tart to cool at room temperature. Once cold remove the overhanging pastry with a knife. Serve with clotted cream.

INGREDIENTS - serves 4-6

For the sweet shortcrust pastry

1. 500g plain flour, sifted
2. 100g icing sugar, sifted
3. 250g cold unsalted butter, cut into small cubes
4. Zest 1 lemon
5. 2 large free range eggs, beaten
6. Splash of iced cold water

For the filling

7. 100g fresh breadcrumbs
8. 350g golden syrup
9. Knob of unsalted butter
10. 1 tsp ground ginger
11. Juice 1/2 lemon
12. 1 large egg, beaten

THE NORMANDY ARMS

Blackawton, Nr Dartmouth, Devon. TEL: 01803 712884

CHEF ROGER HAWKSHAW

The Normandy Arms is situated in Blackawton, a perfect traditional Devon village halfway between Totnes and Dartmouth.

Run by Nick Crosley – a man renowned for his warm welcome to customers, his cooking skills and his ability to have fun with anyone -it has quickly become a big success.

Its menus are created by Roger Hawkshaw, formerly of the renowned, Michelin starred, 'New Angel' and the pub itself reflects the idyllic rural setting with contemporary twists.

Since starting his catering career at the age of 15 when his mum told him to get a job, Roger has certainly come far. He worked with Chris Tanner at Kitley House in Plymouth, and then moved to New York State in America for a couple of years before coming to Dartmouth at the Hooked Restaurant in Higher Street. He then moved to the Carved Angel on the Embankment and shared in its success when it won three Rosettes in 2001.

After leaving the restaurant in 2004, Roger took on a couple of challenges which failed to light his fire, and came back to Dartmouth to help friend Andy Coombe at the Windjammer pub for a year before returning to the New (Carved) Angel with John Burton Race.

Starting in May 2010 Roger has brought his philosophy of cooking to the Normandy Arms, and has been gaining plaudits along the way.

'I like to enjoy what I do – it's terrible when people make food so serious,' he said. 'We are less formal than many restaurants I have worked in, but we don't compromise on the taste and quality of our food. The best ingredients are key to this, and I feel in this smaller kitchen I can be more expressive and enjoy my job.

'Being a chef is a craft, and should be an expression of how you are – I like to make the food both delicious and attractive on the plate, because people do eat with their eyes too!'

METHOD

First rub the Chinese Five Spice into the cheeks and allow to marinade for at least 2 hours. Once ready seal the pigs cheek in a hot pan with some oil (peanut, pomace or vegetable). Don't season as there is plenty in the braising liquor. Colour all over then remove from the pan and place into a roasting tray. Place all the remaining dry ingredients into the same pan you sealed the cheeks in sauté for 2 minutes then add the soy and chicken stock. Bring to boil and pour over the cheeks. Cover in foil and place into a moderate oven, 140°C/ gas 1, for 2.5 – 3 hours. Checking all the time, adding more chicken stock or water if necessary.

Once the cheeks are cooked remove them from the braising liquor and keep warm. Meanwhile strain the cooking liquid through a fine sieve into a saucepan and reduce by a third. Skimming off any fat as it reduces.

When the sauce is ready add back the cheeks. Baste over a low heat. They should be nicely coated with a sticky sauce.

Remove the cheeks and cut into 12 slices (3 each). Place into warmed bowls spooning some of the sauce over.

Lovely served with some stir fried pak choi or Chinese cabbage finished with a little chopped garlic and a few drops of lime juice.

A simple tasty starter using an unused cut of pork.

INGREDIENTS - serves 4

1. **2 pigs cheeks 680g each (skin removed and trimmed, your butcher can do this).**
2. **150g fresh ginger (peeled and chopped)**
3. **1 red chilli (chopped)**
4. **1 tsp coriander (crushed)**
5. **2 star anise**
6. **6 cloves of garlic (sliced)**
7. **50ml light soy sauce**
8. **2 tbsp of cracked black pepper**
9. **500ml chicken stock**
10. **4 banana shallots (peeled and sliced)**
11. **2 tbsp Chinese Five Spice.**

INGREDIENTS - serves 4

1. **4 x 250g Pollack fillet (skin on, de scaled and pin boned, your fishmonger can do this)**

2. **400g celeriac**
   (skinned & chopped into 1 inch dice)

3. **300ml chicken stock**

4. **200ml double cream**

5. **Salt**

6. **White pepper**

7. **10ml white truffle oil (optional)**

8. **12 slices thin pancetta**

9. **200g washed spinach**

10. **10g unsalted butter**

METHOD

Place the chopped celeriac into a sauce pan with the chicken stock and bring to the boil. Simmer over a low heat until the celeriac is tender then add the cream. Continue to cook until the cream is reduced by half. Pour into a liquidizer and blitz until smooth. You can then pass the pureé through a sieve for that extra velvety texture. If for some reason your pureé is too thin you can add it back to a clean pan to further reduce. Be careful! It can be quite volcanic! Once ready, season to taste and add the optional white truffle oil. Reserve somewhere warm.

Cooking the pancetta

Lay out the sliced pancetta onto a baking sheet lined with greaseproof paper. Place another sheet of greaseproof paper on top and another baking sheet on top of that. This method keeps the bacon nice and flat and extra crispy. Place into a pre-headed over at 150ºc/gas 1. Cook for 15-20 minutes. Check constantly through cooking as burnt pancetta isn't very pleasant. Once ready remove the pancetta and place on paper towel to remove excess fat. Your bacon should be crisp and fat; alternatively you could just grill it.

Cooking the fish

Pollack is a very underrated fish, a member of the cod family. It is quite robust and can handle some serious heat and flavouring. Portions from a larger fillet are more desirable but if only small ones are available not to worry. You could always talk to Karl Griffiths, he has some serious pollacks. Season the fish with salt and pepper and place into a hot non stick pan skin side down. Add a drizzle of olive oil and allow to cook on the stove for 2-3 minutes (lower the heat if it starts to smoke!) After 23 minutes place into a pre heated oven 170ºc/gas 3, for a further four minutes. The cooking times may vary due to the thickness of the fish. The thinner the quicker it will cook. Once cooked remove from the oven, baste the fish with the cooking juices, turn over and allow to rest in the pan under a low grill. Saute the spinach in a hot pan with the butter and a little drizzle of oil, season to taste and drain on some kitchen paper to absorb any moisture. In four bowls (warmed) or plates, spoon the celeriac puree into the centre and add the spinach. Top with the fish and pancetta and serve. A drizzle of extra virgin oil will finish the dish.

METHOD

Place the flour, sugar butter and optional vanilla seeds into a bowl or food processor and rub or blend to form a light breadcrumbs texture. Add the egg yolks; this should bring the mixture together. If not then add the reserved water 1 tablespoon at a time until the pastry comes together into a light ball. Wrap in cling film and allow to rest in the fridge for half an hour. This allows the gluten in the flour to relax giving you a much crumblier pastry. After half an hour roll out the pastry on a floured bench. It needs to be large enough to line a 6 inch flan case with room to spare and not too thick (5mm). Wrap the pastry around your rolling pin and line your greased flan case. Don't trim off any excess pastry. Just allow it to hang over the edges. This can be trimmed later. If you trim it now the pastry will shrink back into the flan case when cooking giving you an uneven and shallow pastry case. When the flan case is lined again allow the pastry to rest in the fridge for a further 30 minutes. Meanwhile pre heat your oven to 150°C/gas 1. Line the pastry case with the greaseproof paper add baking beans or uncooked rice and cook in the oven for 20 minutes. Remove the greaseproof and beans and cook for a further 10-15 minutes until the case is golden brown and fully cooked.

Allow to cool. Lower the oven temperature to 100ºC and make the filling.

Place the cream and milk into a saucepan and bring to the boil. Pour over the chocolate and cracked eggs; whisk until a smooth chocolate sauce is achieved.

Pour the chocolate sauce into the flan case and bake in the oven for 20-25 minutes. A simple tap to the tart will allow you to judge the doneness. But if your oven is too hot the mixture will overcook and become grainy and unpleasant.

Once ready place the tart onto your bench and remove the excess pastry. Allow to cool slightly.

Remove from the case and cut into desired portions. Serve with Devon clotted cream.

INGREDIENTS - serves 4-6

Pastry

1. 250g plain flour

2. 125g diced unsalted butter (room temp)

3. 90g sugar

4. 3 large egg yolks

5. 2 tbsp cold water

6. 1 de-seeded vanilla pod (optional)

Filling

1. 175ml double cream

2. 100ml milk

3. 2 whole eggs

4. 250g dark Valrhona chocolate or any other quality dark chocolate (cocoa solids 60-70%).

ROYAL CASTLE HOTEL

11 The Quay, Dartmouth, Devon, TQ6 9PS. TEL: 01803 833033

CHEF RICHARD JENKINS

Richard Jenkins has built up a wealth of experience from some of the best hotels and restaurants in the country. He started his career with an apprenticeship at Claridges Hotel, London gaining a firm footing in the industry and the knowledge of what it takes to be the best. He then moved to the famous Champneys Spa before returning to Devon and the prestigious Thurlestone Hotel. He spent time at the two Rosette Mill End Hotel in Chagford and the one rosette Sampsons Farm before moving to the Grand Hotel, Torquay as executive pastry chef.

'At the Royal Castle we are producing food which I and my team love to cook and the customers love to eat,' he said. 'It is a menu which lives up to my ambitions to produce food which is locally sourced, using the best ingredients, and which is absolutely delicious. People are giving such good feedback we know we have got it right.

'The Westcountry has some of the world's best ingredients on offer and it is a pleasure to use them each day to produce great dishes. It's a pleasure to come to work.'

Nigel Way, has been at the heart of Dartmouth's tourist trade for more than a quarter of a century. Bringing his customary energy and enthusiasm for food and good times to the Royal Castle in the 1980s he and his wife Anne have created a hotel which is as popular with locals as it is with visitors, and he prides himself on keeping his team friendly and attentive to the needs of his customers.

METHOD

In a large sauce pan sauté the onion and garlic until the onion is transparent. Add the chorizo, potatoes, kale and sauté for a further 3-4 minutes. Add the vegetable stock and bring to the boil, simmer until potatoes start to break up and thicken the soup. Season to taste. Serve with crusty bloomer bread.

INGREDIENTS - serves 4

1. 1kg Curly Kale (finely shredded)
2. 500g sliced chorizo
3. 1 medium onion finely diced
4. 2 medium potatoes cut into 1 inch cubes
5. 2 cloves of crushed garlic
6. 1 ltr veg stock or hot water

INGREDIENTS - serves 4

For the suet paste

1. 500g self raising flour
2. 250g shredded beef suet
3. 275ml water (approx)
4. Pinch of salt and freshly ground black pepper

For the filling

5. 800g diced chuck steak
6. 100g porcini/cep mushrooms
7. 1 bay leaf
8. 2 shallots, sliced
9. 60g plain flour
10. 1 tbsp Worcester sauce
11. Salt and pepper
12. 150ml beef stock

METHOD

Grease a 1.75 litres/ 3 pint pudding bowl with butter.

For the pastry, sift the flour into a bowl. Add the suet and season, with salt and fresh black pepper. Gradually add the water, mixing well; until the mixture comes together like dough (you may not need all the water). Turn out dough onto a lightly floured surface and divide off a quarter and set aside. Roll the remaining dough into a circle approx 10cm round. Transfer the pastry to the greased pudding bowl and mould it to the sides leaving excess pastry hanging over the bowl edge. Roll the other piece of dough into a circle approx 1cm thick and 2.5cm wider than the top of the pudding bowl, set to one side. For the filling, mix together all ingredients, except for the stock, and season with the salt and pepper to taste, spoon into lined pudding bowl and pour over the stock.

Place the pastry lid on top of the pudding basin, moisten the edges and press down to seal.

Place a sheet of non stick parchment paper on top and then wrap the pudding basin in tin foil, secure with string. Transfer the bowl into a large saucepan and add enough water to reach halfway up the sides of the pudding bowl, cover the pan with a lid and steam for 5 hours, adding more water as and when necessary.

Serve with new potatoes and roasted root vegetables.

METHOD

Whisk the egg yolks, honey and sugar until well combined, add cream and rosemary.

Leave over night to infuse.

Pass through a fine sieve and pour into oven proof ramekins (110ml), place onto a baking tray and cook for approx 1 hour at 100°C until set (mixture should still wobble slightly if shaken)

Allow to set fully in the fridge

Lightly dust with Demerara sugar and glaze with a blow torch (or under the grill). Serve with Scottish highland shortbreads.

INGREDIENTS - serves 4-6

1. **10 egg yolks**
2. **100g caster sugar**
3. **1 litre double cream**
4. **Fresh rosemary**
5. **Demerara sugar (to glaze)**

TAYLOR'S RESTAURANT

8 The Quay, Dartmouth, Devon TQ6 9PS. TEL: 01803 832748

CHEF PETER SHAW

Taylor's Chef & Proprietor, Peter Shaw, has been a chef for more years than he can remember, having been encouraged to join the industry by his older cousin at the age of 16.

After training at the Old Government House Hotel in Guernsey, his career took him to various country house hotels, the Amsterdam Marriot and to the House of Commons. Before buying Taylor's in 1999 he worked for several years at the head office of Diageo plc in London as a Director's chef which enabled him to showcase his talents with elaborate dinners prepared for Royalty and various heads of state.

Taylor's Restaurant is situated on the Quay in Dartmouth overlooking the Boatfloat and has been run by both Peter and his partner Pauline

Shapland for 12 years. The views of the harbour and town are stunning and it's probably the best place in town for people watching!

Taylor's is renowned for good old fashioned cooking, with fresh fish and shellfish a speciality. Sparkling chandeliers and gorgeous artwork sets the scene for a cosy, relaxed and intimate dining experience making Taylor's a firm favourite with locals and holidaymakers alike.

The dishes Peter has prepared for this book are dishes he cooked for friends on board his yacht during various sailing trips so they are relatively simple and easy to prepare afloat as well as in the home.

METHOD

Peel the garlic and boil until soft. Open up the box of Camembert and without removing it from its box and wrapper, make a couple of incisions into the cheese and slip in a clove of garlic per incision. Drizzle with Calvados to taste. Bake whole in the box in a moderate oven for 30 minutes. Garnish with some fried apple slices and garlic cloves and serve with the crusty bread, some sliced apples for dipping and a crisp salad.

INGREDIENTS - serves 4

1. 1 Camembert in a box
2. Crusty bread
3. Cloves of garlic to taste
4. Sliced apples for dipping (optional)
5. Calvados (optional)

INGREDIENTS - serves 4

1. 800g fresh filleted halibut, cut into 4 steaks, floured and seasoned

2. 4 handfuls of wild mushrooms cleaned and wiped, such as ceps, oyster, chanterelles, trumpets, shiitake

3. 4 tbsp olive oil for frying

4. 50g butter

5. Clove of garlic (optional)

6. Whole lemon, cut into 4 wedges

7. White truffle oil

8. Chopped parsley (for garnish)

METHOD

Pan-fry the halibut steaks for two minutes either side in half the olive oil (fry with skin side down first).

Remove from pan, allow to rest and keep warm.

In the remainder of oil, melt the butter and gently fry the garlic and the mushrooms.

Serve the halibut onto plates, with skin side down and sprinkle with equal quantities of the mushrooms & cooking juices. Drizzle with white truffle oil, garnish with chopped parsley and serve with a lemon wedge and some simple vegetables such as new potatoes and wilted spinach.

METHOD

Place each banana in a large square of tin foil, big enough to hold each banana. Drizzle with maple syrup, sprinkle with crumbled chocolate, sultanas and crushed hazelnuts and seal up as long parcels. Cook in a hot oven for 15 minutes. Serve with clotted cream and/ or ice cream..

INGREDIENTS - serves 4

1. 4 bananas
2. Jar of maple syrup
3. Small handful of crushed hazelnuts
4. Some crumbled cooking chocolate
5. Soaked sultanas (boil in some water & simmer for a few mins.)
6. Clotted cream and / or ice cream for serving

Dartmouth Caring is looking to attract new people to join their ever expanding membership scheme. The more members who join us help support the important work we do as a charity in the local community.

Our membership scheme is open to anyone, young and old, able or infirm, and offers financial assistance to the charity as well as the twice yearly opportunity for someone to win the substantial prize draw fund. You will also receive our newsletter updating you on what the charity is doing. There is no other obligation by members. The draws are held in June and December and winner takes all! The last prize was for £880. The annual membership fee is £20.00 of which £10.00 is a direct contribution to the vital work of the charity and the other £10.00 is deposited into the draw fund. If you

are a UK tax payer we can also claim back a further £2.50 through Gift Aid; please tick the box. Dartmouth Caring is funded almost entirely by charitable donations and by signing up to the membership scheme you will become part of a valued community and help to support a range of services that enable the elderly and the vulnerable in Dartmouth and the surrounding villages to remain as independent as possible.

To join please call into our office for an application form opposite the surgery, or telephone 01803 835384 and we can pop one in the post. Alternatively email us on enquiries@dartmouthcaring.co.uk or visit our web site dartmouthcaring.co.uk where a form can be downloaded. Please do contact us and join!

We look forward to hearing from you soon.

Dartmouth Caring
Supporting Our Community